T0194665

An Analysis of

Douglas McGregor's

The Human Side
of Enterprise

Stoyan Stoyanov
with
Monique Diderich

Published by Macat International Ltd
24:13 Coda Centre, 189 Munster Road, London SW6 6AW.

Dristributed exclusively by Routledge
2 Park Square, Milton Park, Abingdon, Oxon OX14 4RN
711 Third Avenue, New York, NY 10017, USA

Routledge is an imprint of the Taylor & Francis Group, an informa business

www.macat.com
info@macat.com

Cataloguing in Publication Data
A catalogue record for this book is available from the British Library.
Library of Congress Cataloguing-in-Publication Data is available upon request.
Cover illustration: Etienne Gilfillan

ISBN 978-1-912302-17-8 (hardback)
ISBN 978-1-912128-18-1 (paperback)
ISBN 978-1-912281-05-3 (e-book)

Notice
The information in this book is designed to orientate readers of the work under analysis,
to elucidate and contextualise its key ideas and themes, and to aid in the development
of critical thinking skills. It is not meant to be used, nor should it be used, as a
substitute for original thinking or in place of original writing or research. References and
notes are provided for informational purposes and their presence does not constitute
endorsement of the information or opinions therein. This book is presented solely for
educational purposes. It is sold on the understanding that the publisher is not engaged
to provide any scholarly advice. The publisher has made every effort to ensure that
this book is accurate and up-to-date, but makes no warranties or representations with
regard to the completeness or reliability of the information it contains. The information
and the opinions provided herein are not guaranteed or warranted to produce particular
results and may not be suitable for students of every ability. The publisher shall not be
liable for any loss, damage or disruption arising from any errors or omissions, or from
the use of this book, including, but not limited to, special, incidental, consequential or
other damages caused, or alleged to have been caused, directly or indirectly, by the
information contained within.

CONTENTS

THE MACAT LIBRARY

The Macat Library is a series of unique academic explorations of seminal works in the humanities and social sciences – books and papers that have had a significant and widely recognised impact on their disciplines. It has been created to serve as much more than just a summary of what lies between the covers of a great book. It illuminates and explores the influences on, ideas of, and impact of that book. Our goal is to offer a learning resource that encourages critical thinking and fosters a better, deeper understanding of important ideas.

Each publication is divided into three Sections: Influences, Ideas, and Impact. Each Section has four Modules. These explore every important facet of the work, and the responses to it.

This Section-Module structure makes a Macat Library book easy to use, but it has another important feature. Because each Macat book is written to the same format, it is possible (and encouraged!) to cross-reference multiple Macat books along the same lines of inquiry or research. This allows the reader to open up interesting interdisciplinary pathways.

To further aid your reading, lists of glossary terms and people mentioned are included at the end of this book (these are indicated by an asterisk [*] throughout) – as well as a list of works cited.

Macat has worked with the University of Cambridge to identify the elements of critical thinking and understand the ways in which six different skills combine to enable effective thinking.
Three allow us to fully understand a problem; three more give us the tools to solve it. Together, these six skills make up the **PACIER** model of critical thinking. They are:

ANALYSIS – understanding how an argument is built
EVALUATION – exploring the strengths and weaknesses of an argument
INTERPRETATION – understanding issues of meaning

CREATIVE THINKING – coming up with new ideas and fresh connections
PROBLEM-SOLVING – producing strong solutions
REASONING – creating strong arguments

To find out more, visit **WWW.MACAT.COM.**

CRITICAL THINKING AND *THE HUMAN SIDE OF ENTERPRISE*

Primary critical thinking skill: EVALUATION
Secondary critical thinking skill: REASONING

What makes a good manager? Though we can probably all point to someone we think of as a good manager, what precisely makes them so good at their job is a complex question – and one central to good business organization. Management scholar Douglas McGregor's seminal 1960 book *The Human Side of Enterprise* is perhaps the most influential attempt to answer that question, and provides an excellent example of strong evaluative and reasoning skills in action.

Evaluation is a critical thinking skill that requires judging the strength and weakness of positions: a critical evaluation asks how acceptable a line of reasoning is, and how adequate, relevant and convincing the evidence is. McGregor sought to find out what makes a good manager by evaluating different management approaches, their assumptions about human behavior, and effects they had. In his view, management approaches could be roughly broken down into two 'theories': Theory X, which held a negative idea of employee motivations; and Theory Y, which made positive assumptions about them. McGregor's evaluation showed that Theory Y produced markedly better results in productivity and other measurable areas. On this basis, McGregor reasoned out a strong, persuasive argument for adopting Theory Y strategies on a grand scale.

ABOUT THE AUTHOR OF THE ORIGINAL WORK

Douglas McGregor was born in Detroit in the United States in 1906. As a young man, he witnessed the effects of the Great Depression—the economic downturn of the 1930s. McGregor wanted to improve the lives of those who experience adversity and try to understand the kind of conditions that could make work enjoyable and meaningful. He received his doctorate from Harvard in 1935, and was eventually hired by the prestigious Massachusetts Institute of Technology. As a faculty member specializing in social and organizational psychology, McGregor dedicated his career to studying what makes work satisfying, and his thinking has had a great influence on business scholars. Douglas McGregor died in 1964 at the age of 58.

ABOUT THE AUTHORS OF THE ANALYSIS

Dr Stoyan Stoyanov holds a PhD in management from the University of Edinburgh. He is currently a lecturer at the Hunter Centre for Entrepreneurship at the University of Strathclyde, Glasgow.

Dr Monique Diderich holds a masters degree in psychology from the University of Groningen and a doctorate in sociology from the University of Nevada, Las Vegas.

ABOUT MACAT

GREAT WORKS FOR CRITICAL THINKING

Macat is focused on making the ideas of the world's great thinkers accessible and comprehensible to everybody, everywhere, in ways that promote the development of enhanced critical thinking skills.

It works with leading academics from the world's top universities to produce new analyses that focus on the ideas and the impact of the most influential works ever written across a wide variety of academic disciplines. Each of the works that sit at the heart of its growing library is an enduring example of great thinking. But by setting them in context – and looking at the influences that shaped their authors, as well as the responses they provoked – Macat encourages readers to look at these classics and game-changers with fresh eyes. Readers learn to think, engage and challenge their ideas, rather than simply accepting them.

'Macat offers an amazing first-of-its-kind tool for interdisciplinary learning and research. Its focus on works that transformed their disciplines and its rigorous approach, drawing on the world's leading experts and educational institutions, opens up a world-class education to anyone.'

Andreas Schleicher
Director for Education and Skills, Organisation for Economic Co-operation and Development

'Macat is taking on some of the major challenges in university education … They have drawn together a strong team of active academics who are producing teaching materials that are novel in the breadth of their approach.'

Prof Lord Broers,
former Vice-Chancellor of the University of Cambridge

'The Macat vision is exceptionally exciting. It focuses upon new modes of learning which analyse and explain seminal texts which have profoundly influenced world thinking and so social and economic development. It promotes the kind of critical thinking which is essential for any society and economy. This is the learning of the future.'

Rt Hon Charles Clarke, former UK Secretary of State for Education

'The Macat analyses provide immediate access to the critical conversation surrounding the books that have shaped their respective discipline, which will make them an invaluable resource to all of those, students and teachers, working in the field.'

Professor William Tronzo, University of California at San Diego

WAYS IN TO THE TEXT

KEY POINTS

- Douglas McGregor (1906–64) grew up in the early twentieth century. When he was young, he witnessed firsthand the struggle of those searching for work in the worldwide financial crisis known as the Great Depression.*

- Studying the ways in which different organizations manage their employees led him to develop a novel management style, Theory Y,* founded on the idea that people are self-motivated and do not need to be strictly controlled.

- McGregor's *The Human Side of Enterprise* (1960) is one of the most influential books about management of the twentieth century.

Who Was Douglas McGregor?

Douglas McGregor, the author of *The Human Side of Enterprise* (1960), was born in 1906 in Detroit, Michigan, in the United States. Growing up, he witnessed the Great Depression (the decade following the 1929 collapse of the US stock market, which led to unemployment and impoverishment for millions worldwide). He also saw that even when there was employment, wages were not always enough to pay for food and housing. In these years, McGregor had the opportunity to work for his family's charitable organization, where he met people who were living in poverty and struggling to provide for their families. Together, these experiences greatly influenced his career and his interest in the conditions in which people worked best.

In 1935, McGregor received his doctorate in psychology from Harvard University. He then taught briefly at Harvard before eventually becoming a faculty member at the prestigious Massachusetts Institute of Technology (MIT). McGregor's work as an organizational psychologist*—someone engaged in the systematic study of how the workplace affects the human mind—focused on working conditions and employee well-being. He also studied how working conditions could be made more satisfying for workers.

McGregor lived during a period of great change for businesses. He witnessed the emergence of many large enterprises and organizations, and the advent of numerous technical innovations. These innovations allowed corporations to drastically increase their production of goods—and they had a similarly dramatic effect on what was required of workers. His observations eventually led to *The Human Side of Enterprise*, published in 1960. Only four years later, at the relatively young age of 58, he died of a heart attack.

What Does *The Human Side of Enterprise* Say?

In his book, McGregor writes that a management style is based on how managers see their employees. He compares and contrasts two views in particular, which he calls Theory X* and Theory Y, and describes how they influence efficiency and productivity.

Theory X, the traditional theory of management, is based on the belief that human beings are lazy by nature and will not work hard without being rewarded. According to McGregor, managers with a Theory X mind-set believe in strict measures for controlling employees and rely on a system of rewards and punishments:

employees receive rewards for good performance and are punished if they work poorly. This approach does not account for the importance of trust in human relationships.

By comparison, Theory Y recognizes that employees have goals, and attempts to integrate these goals with those of the organization. This means that employees work with management toward the success of the enterprise.

Theory Y also assumes that individuals do not work to fulfill basic needs alone: they also want to develop social relationships and camaraderie with their colleagues. For these reasons, readers should see his approach as being rooted in humanism,* a philosophy that values the individual's desire to learn and to fulfill his or her creative potential.

Unlike Theory X, Theory Y builds on the American psychologist Abraham Maslow's* "hierarchy of needs,"* a model of human behavior that describes how people are motivated by praise and the desire to learn. Employees work better, McGregor argues, when they are able to learn and take pride in their work. He believes that satisfied employees are productive employees, and he advocates collaboration between employees and managers. *The Human Side of Enterprise* is a guide for organizations that want to abandon a management style informed by Theory X in favor of one informed by Theory Y.

McGregor hoped that his book would inspire managers to reflect on their assumptions about human behavior and on how those assumptions influence their interactions with employees, and would show them how to set goals that take into account employee satisfaction. He also wanted to inspire academics who study management to build theories that fit modern businesses better.

Why Does *The Human Side of Enterprise* Matter?
McGregor examines how good managers motivate their employees

to take an interest in the goals of their employers (rather than concerning themselves with simply receiving a paycheck). He suggests that good managers have a better understanding of what drives human behavior.

McGregor also investigates many contemporary assumptions about how employees should be treated. For example, he argues that individual employees should not be blamed when an organization is unproductive or unprofitable. Under McGregor's Theory Y, the manager is to blame for failing to adapt to their employees' specific needs. Managers are also responsible for their employees' professional growth and learning.

McGregor's writing is clear and engaging, which makes it possible for people other than academics—managers in the business world, for instance—to understand the practical implications of Theory Y. *The Human Side of Enterprise* is also a guide: McGregor devotes more than a hundred pages to describing how organizations can begin to work on Theory Y assumptions.

Organizations that use McGregor's Theory Y are often called learning organizations* because they are able to transform themselves through helping their employees learn and grow. These organizations often value personal mastery, shared vision, and team learning. Similarly, McGregor's work also laid the groundwork for contingency theories* that were developed after his death. Contingency theories describe how management and leadership must adapt and change depending on the state of the markets in which they operate.

The Human Side of Enterprise was the most important work of McGregor's life. Even today, it remains among the most influential books written on management.

SECTION 1
INFLUENCES

MODULE 1
THE AUTHOR AND THE
HISTORICAL CONTEXT

KEY POINTS

- *The Human Side of Enterprise* has been declared one of the most significant works of the twentieth century by the Academy of Management, publisher of the highly respected *Academy of Management Journal.*

- When he was young, McGregor worked for his family's McGregor Institute,* a charitable organization that assisted those who were unemployed or disadvantaged.

- His experiences with the McGregor Institute encouraged him to dedicate his career to helping impoverished people.

Why Read This Text?

In *The Human Side of Enterprise* (1960), Douglas McGregor introduces his vision for modern working conditions. He compares this vision to a more traditional way of managing employees, arguing that his humanistic* approach (an approach that values the human experience) will lead to more effective and efficient managerial practices.

According to McGregor, a management style that treats employees as lazy and in need of strict control does not reflect human behavior and motivation accurately. He argues that those who study management should draw more on research from the field of social sciences: "I share with some of my colleagues the conviction that the social sciences could contribute more effectively than they have to managerial progress with respect to the human side of enterprise."[1]

> ❝ Behind every managerial decision or action are assumptions about human nature and human behavior. ❞
>
> Douglas McGregor, *The Human Side of Enterprise*

He also emphasizes that managers themselves should be aware of advancements in knowledge about human behavior. As he puts it: "The professional need not be a scientist, but he must be sophisticated enough to make competent use of scientific knowledge."[2]

McGregor believed that employees naturally want to do good work. This motivation comes from taking pride in their accomplishments and satisfying their responsibilities. Based on research in the social sciences that has highlighted the human need for growth and learning, McGregor called for the development of a new management theory in which managers see their employees as human resources.

When managers acknowledge their employees' need for growth, McGregor showed, they also encourage learning, and participation with and for the organization as a whole. Unfortunately, at the time, employers did not see their employees in this way; as McGregor put it, "conventional managerial strategies for the organization, direction, and control of the human resources of enterprise are admirably suited to the capacities and characteristics of the child rather than the adult."[3]

McGregor expressed and defended his views so successfully that he soon became regarded as one of the most significant contributors to the field of organizational development* (an academic field of study focused on understanding and managing how large entities, like companies and corporations, change and evolve). *The Human Side of Enterprise* has been an important reference for generations of scholars, and today has been cited approximately 10,000 times.

Author's Life

McGregor was born in 1906 in Detroit, Michigan. When he was young, he worked for the McGregor Institute,* a charitable organization founded by his grandfather in 1895. The Institute's mission was to help those who were struggling to find work or who could not sustain themselves on the work they could find. As well as providing food and shelter for around a thousand people each year, it offered direction and religious support. His work with the Institute helped McGregor become aware of the issues that working people faced.

McGregor attended City College of Detroit (now Wayne State University) and Oberlin College in Ohio. He then attended the prestigious psychology program at Harvard University, where in 1935 he earned his PhD. He worked at Harvard for two years before being hired by the Massachusetts Institute of Technology (MIT) as the first faculty member specializing in social psychology (the scientific study of the workings of the mind in a social context).[4]

In addition to his career at MIT, McGregor worked as a consultant with a rubber and sealants company. He helped negotiate contracts and train foremen; he also handled grievances and advised as to how the organization should be structured. This allowed him to test and apply his theories in the real world.

In 1948, McGregor became president of Antioch College, a progressive university in Yellow Springs, Ohio—one of the first mainstream colleges in the United States to accept African American students. Six years later, McGregor returned to MIT, where he became a faculty member of the Sloan School of Management.[5] It was during this time at MIT that McGregor helped found the academic field of organizational development in the late 1950s and early 1960s.[6] He died in 1964 of a heart attack, four years after the publication of *The Human Side of Enterprise.*

Author's Background

McGregor came of age in Detroit, a city that would become one of the nation's leading industrial centers and the automobile capital of the world.[7] During his childhood, the assembly line was invented and was put to use in factories. The assembly line had an enormous effect on businesses, as it allowed for the mass production of goods. It changed the very nature of work; instead of working on one car at a time, workers were assigned specialized tasks that affected a small part of a car's overall production.

McGregor's career was also shaped by the Great Depression* of the 1930s—a grave financial crisis that saw millions lose their jobs and face poverty. McGregor worked for his family's Institute during the early years of the Depression, helping to provide temporary accommodation for migrant workers.[8] McGregor would note later that while part-time workers and the unemployed struggled during the Depression, "Management was [also] subjected to severe pressures."[9]

McGregor had a close relationship with his father, who was also involved with the Institute. During his life, they exchanged letters in which they discussed their philosophies. Though they were both compassionate, McGregor believed more strongly than his father in people's innate goodness.

NOTES

1   Douglas McGregor, *The Human Side of Enterprise* (New York: McGraw-Hill, 1960), 5.

2   McGregor, *Human Side of Enterprise*, 5.

3   McGregor, *Human Side of Enterprise*, 43.

4   MIT Sloan School of Management, "Pioneered at MIT Sloan," accessed November 19, 2015, http://mitsloan.mit.edu/faculty/spotlight/pioneered.php.

5   Managers-Net, "Douglas McGregor," accessed November 19, 2015, www.managers-net.com/Biography/mcgregor.html

6   MIT Sloan, "Pioneered at MIT Sloan."

7   McGregor Fund, "History," accessed November 19, 2015, www.mcgregorfund.org/about-us/history.

8   Managers-Net, "Douglas McGregor."

9   McGregor, *Human Side of Enterprise*, 46.

MODULE 2
ACADEMIC CONTEXT

KEY POINTS

- Traditionally, the primary method of industrial management was informed by the principles of scientific management,* an approach founded on the assumption that employees can be managed along scientific lines.

- The working conditions of any business are determined by managers' assumptions about human nature and what motivates employees.

- In 1954, a grant from the nonprofit Alfred P. Sloan Foundation,* which provides grants for education and research into science and technology, gave McGregor and his colleagues an opportunity to conduct systematic study into what makes a good manager.

The Work in its Context

Douglas McGregor's *The Human Side of Enterprise* responded to the existing consensus on management techniques. During the early twentieth century, managers exerted strict control over their employees, telling them what to do, and how and when to do it. Workers were rewarded or punished based on how well they performed in these circumstances; poor performance could result in a worker being fired.

Managers were often scrutinized by upper management; McGregor observed, for example, that many big corporations required managers to have annual physical examinations, and data based on these physicals were then used in decisions about that manager's future—whether or not he or she should be promoted,

> **❝** Classical organization theory suffers from 'ethnocentrism': it ignores the significance of the political, social, and economic milieu in shaping organizations and influencing managerial practice. **❞**
>
> Douglas McGregor, *The Human Side of Enterprise*

for example.[1] McGregor believed this showed that corporations exerted excessive control over both employees and managers.

As a consequence of these conditions, American society in the 1930s and 1940s was concerned with the ethics of managerial policies. Important regulations about child labor, employment of women, workers' compensation, and the right to collective bargaining (when laborers organize themselves to negotiate with their employers collectively) were being considered and passed. These restrictions obstructed a manager's freedom to exert control over employees, and were typically viewed by managers as unreasonable, but they ultimately improved working conditions. By the 1950s, workers enjoyed higher standards of living, and employers were paying more attention to what sorts of working conditions could improve employee job satisfaction.[2]

Overview of the Field

In the early twentieth century, management practices were rooted in the scientific management principles of Frederick Winslow Taylor,* a nineteenth-century engineer. Taylor's views on management, control, and the organization of work significantly influenced many corporations of his time.

An important aspect of Taylor's managerial theory is that workers should work faster and thereby generate greater output. Taylor studied factory workers, timing them with a stopwatch to see how long it took them to accomplish a particular task. He believed that the standard should be set by the worker whose productivity was fastest.

Holding workers to such standards became widely adopted, especially once technological innovations such as the assembly line were implemented and workers began to perform smaller, repetitive tasks. Taylor predicted that increasing worker productivity would lead to higher profits for the company, which in turn would lead to higher wages for employees.

Taylor's theory was based on his belief that people have a "natural instinct and tendency … to take it easy, which may be called natural soldiering."*[3] Working slowly, he argued, causes fellow workers who would otherwise work hard to also work slowly—a concept Taylor called "systematic soldiering."* Systematic soldiering threatens an organization's profits, since it has a negative effect on production.

Academic Influences

McGregor's training in psychology inspired him to draw on fellow psychologists in exploring group dynamics* (the study of how people behave in groups), a field of study that dates as far back as the1930s. One particularly important figure in group dynamics was Kurt Lewin,* a German American psychologist who studied leadership and how it influences group performance. According to the development consultant Anthony Lerner,* Lewin and his colleagues "were not guided merely by intellectual curiosity. They were guided by a sense of urgency to better understand aspects of group behavior that fostered democracy and individual choice in participation."[4]

McGregor was also influenced by the intellectual culture at MIT. In the early 1950s, during a meeting of the Advisory Committee of MIT's School of Industrial Management, the wealthy automotive business executive Alfred Sloan* posed questions about successful managers that encouraged McGregor to engage in systematic research into different management styles; in 1954, he received a grant from Sloan's nonprofit Sloan Foundation that enabled him to do so.

McGregor was also influenced by those he worked with, such as the management scholar Theodore M. Alfred,* who was one of his graduate students. Their joint study, in which they interviewed managers,[5] laid the groundwork for *The Human Side of Enterprise*. It is likely that McGregor also shared knowledge with Alex Bavelas,* an American psychologist and professor of business management, and another faculty member at MIT.

NOTES

1   Douglas McGregor, *The Human Side of Enterprise* (New York: McGraw-Hill, 1960), 13.

2   McGregor, *Human Side of Enterprise*, 12.

3   Frederick Winslow Taylor, "Fundamentals of Scientific Management," in *Working in America: Continuity, Conflict, and Change*, ed. Amy S. Wharton (Mountain View, CA: Mayfield Publishing Company, 1998), 67–75.

4   Arthur Lerner, "McGregor's Legacy: Thoughts on What He Left, What Transpired, and What Remains to Pursue," *Journal of Management History* 17, no. 2 (2011): 219.

5   McGregor, *Human Side of Enterprise*, v.

MODULE 3
THE PROBLEM

KEY POINTS

- Managers' assumptions about human behavior decide how they treat their subordinates.
- Management styles of the early to mid-twentieth century were based on faulty understandings of human behavior.
- Traditional organizational theory reflected neither current understandings about technology nor social science research into human behavior.

Core Question

During a meeting of the Advisory Council of the School of Industrial Management at MIT, the businessman Alfred Sloan* articulated two questions that would become important for McGregor: What makes a successful manager? And are "successful managers born or made?"[1]

In 1954 a grant from the Sloan Foundation* (an organization founded to support research and education in innovative science and technology) allowed McGregor to pursue these questions by examining manager training programs in a variety of large companies to "learn more about the way in which theories and practices within different organizations influence the making of managers."[2] The study also tried to determine what kinds of people have the ability to become managers, as well as how employers can encourage their employees to learn and grow.

McGregor studied what managers actually did on a day-to-day basis; he observed their interactions with both their own managers and their subordinates. He determined that managers' assumptions about human behavior greatly influenced their interactions with their subordinates.

> ❝ If there is a single assumption which pervades conventional organizational theory it is that authority is the central, indispensable means of managerial control. This is the basic principle of organization in the textbook theory of management. The very structure of the organization is a hierarchy of authoritative relationships. ❞
>
> Douglas McGregor, *The Human Side of Enterprise*

As a result, he conducted a systematic study of assumptions held by top managers about "the most effective way to manage people."[3]

McGregor's book therefore addresses four core questions:

- What makes a good manager?
- What are managers' assumptions about human nature?
- Are these assumptions correct or false?
- Are recent developments within the social sciences applied in organizations?

The Participants

Douglas McGregor was a proponent of humanistic* management—a philosophy that values individual growth and learning. He was inspired by psychologists such as Kurt Lewin,* who explored group dynamics* in the 1930s. He also drew on other scholars, such as the social worker Mary Parker Follett,* who is seen as a pioneer in organizational behavior, the Australian psychologist Elton Mayo,* who specialized in group dynamics, and the psychologist Abraham Maslow,* who developed an important model of human behavior known as Maslow's hierarchy of needs.*[4]

McGregor learned from Mayo that workers value belonging to a group more than they value monetary rewards. Mayo also argued that worker satisfaction was dependent on cooperation and socialization within the working environment. That is, he claimed that workers who are socially satisfied are also more productive.[5]

McGregor's theoretical underpinning came from Abraham Maslow's *A Theory of Human Motivation*, which describes Maslow's hierarchy of needs and his concept of self-actualization* (a person's desire to develop his or her creative potential).[6] McGregor based his argument for the sort of perspective on human behavior that managers should have on Maslow's hierarchy.

In Maslow's hierarchy, human needs are broken down into different levels. At the bottom are physiological needs: the need for food and shelter. Next come safety needs: the need to live and work in a safe environment. These are followed by social needs: the need for meaningful relationships and meaningful work. Next are esteem needs: needs related to self-respect and self-confidence. And at the top of the hierarchy are self-actualization needs—those relating to reaching one's full creative potential.

While traditional management strategies only concerned themselves with physiological and safety needs, the bottom two levels, McGregor proposed that management should also aim to satisfy the higher-level needs, and that doing so would lead to higher job satisfaction and increased productivity.

The Contemporary Debate

At the beginning of the twentieth century, there was an important debate within the social sciences about the future of organizational theory. The classical theorists, who adopted the notion of Sigmund Freud* (often called the father of psychoanalysis)* that human beings are idle by nature and will not work hard unless controlled and incentivized,[7] were often at odds with those in the field of behavioral management,* initially developed by the American psychologists John B. Watson* and B. F. Skinner.*[8] Behavioral management theorists believed that management practices should account for the human need for growth and learning.

The postwar period*—a period of adjustment during which millions of soldiers returned home from fighting in World War II— allowed researchers to study how organizations structure themselves and manage their employees. During this time, McGregor and others who aligned themselves with behavioral management challenged the scientific management* theories that stipulated that workers need to be strictly controlled.

Behavioral management theorists like McGregor and management consultant Peter Drucker* applied humanistic values to management and organizational leadership. McGregor himself was able to use his training in psychology to critique classical management principles. He introduced important psychological concepts that applied human motivation and behavior to employee development, and also studied the extent to which knowledge derived from the social sciences could be implemented in various organizations.

NOTES

1   Douglas McGregor, *The Human Side of Enterprise* (New York: McGraw-Hill, 1960), v.

2   McGregor, *Human Side of Enterprise*, vi.

3   McGregor, *Human Side of Enterprise*, vii.

4   Abraham Maslow, "A Theory of Human Motivation," *Psychological Review* 50 (1943): 370– 96; Abraham Maslow, *Motivation and Personality* (New York: Harper & Row, 1954).

5   Managers-Net, "George Elton Mayo," accessed November 20, 2015, www.managers-net.com/Biography/Mayo.html.

6   Maslow, "Human Motivation," 370–96.

7   Sigmund Freud, "An Outline of Psycho-analysis," *International Journal of Psychoanalysis* 21 (1940): 27–84.

8   John B. Watson, "Psychology as the Behaviorist Views It," *Psychological Review* 20 (1913): 158–77.

MODULE 4
THE AUTHOR'S CONTRIBUTION

KEY POINTS

- McGregor focused on a systematic analysis of contemporary management styles and their effectiveness within organizations.

- McGregor wanted to draw the attention of those working in management to new psychological understandings about human motivation.

- He believed that these new psychological understandings could form the basis for new management strategies and practices.

Author's Aims

Douglas McGregor, the author of *The Human Side of Enterprise*, spent his career trying to understand the complicated ways in which organizations work and are structured; he wanted to learn whether or not working conditions could be designed to accommodate both the company's objectives and their employees' personal needs. Previously, it had been thought that authority, hierarchy, and control were key to motivating people to work. Key principles developed by psychologists about human motivation, and seeing people as resources, had not yet been adopted.

McGregor wanted to demonstrate that these traditional management strategies were based on obsolete notions about human behavior, and that they hampered efficiency and productivity. Referring to these strategies, he wrote, "We will be unlikely to improve our managerial competence by blaming people for failing to behave according to our predictions."[1] That is, companies using

> **❝ It will be clear to the reader that I believe many of our present assumptions about the most effective way to manage people are far from adequate. ❞**
>
> Douglas McGregor, *The Human Side of Enterprise*

traditional management practices should not blame their employees when those practices fail to produce results.

In addition to adopting principles from the field of psychology, McGregor also wanted to develop a management theory firmly rooted in humanism,* a philosophy that values individual human beings and their right to realize their full potential.

McGregor's theories helped modernize the way in which businesses structure themselves and view their employees. He helped promote the idea that taking a more humane view of workers not only improves their satisfaction, but also increases productivity.

Approach

McGregor's approach included an analysis of management styles within organizations. He systematically studied prevailing assumptions about human behavior within the organizational context; specifically, he wanted to make the case that organizations whose view of human behavior was derived from the work of Sigmund Freud,* and from the "scientific" theories of the early management scholar Frederick Winslow Taylor,* do not offer their workers an environment conducive to effectiveness, efficiency, and productivity. Those organizations do not fully use the potential of their human resources.

McGregor was certain that psychological and social science research could contribute to more effective methods of management—methods that would benefit both employers *and* employees. He built on the work of the organizational theorist and industrial researcher Elton Mayo* and the psychologist Abraham Maslow* to show that working in groups makes people happier and more productive.

Throughout *The Human Side of Enterprise*, McGregor argues that managers should examine how their assumptions about human behavior affect the way they treat their subordinates. McGregor's insights helped organizations create more satisfying and efficient working conditions so that both they and their employees could thrive.

Contribution in Context

McGregor was among the first to express suspicion about how employees had traditionally been supervised, and to argue that management needed to adjust its view of human ability. Even after this view became popularized, however, McGregor's work stood out from that of his peers; he was able to combine important research from various fields and present it in a way that was easy to understand.

McGregor described two main theories of management, which he called Theory X* and Theory Y.* Theory X, the traditional theory, assumed that people were lazy and needed to be strictly controlled or rewarded depending on their performance. According to Theory Y, people want to experience growth not only financially, but intellectually and emotionally. McGregor argued that modern businesses should shift away from Theory X practices, and proposed Theory Y as an alternative.

It was also important for McGregor that managers consider their own styles and beliefs about people before adopting a new approach. Theory X styles reflected a negative stance on human motivation. Managers who ascribed to these traditional practices did not account for self-initiative* (the ability of employees to begin projects without being told to do so by their managers) and trust in the workplace. As McGregor described it: "People, deprived of opportunities to satisfy at work the needs which are now important to them, behave exactly as we might predict—with indolence, passivity, unwillingness to accept responsibility, resistance to change ... [and] unreasonable demands for economic benefits. It would seem that we may be caught in a web of our own weaving."[2] Theory X management practices, he believed, led to poor productivity and unsatisfied workers.

McGregor's alternative approach to managing workers, Theory Y, attempted to account for Elton Mayo's discovery that people like working in groups, and for Abraham Maslow's hierarchy of needs,* a psychological model that described a range of motivations for human behavior. McGregor wrote that "Unless there are opportunities *at work* to satisfy these higher-level needs, people will be deprived; and their behavior will reflect this deprivation."[3]

To avoid feeling deprived, McGregor believed, employees need to feel that their work is meaningful, and that they have the respect and fellowship of their colleagues. They also gain satisfaction from learning and collaborating.

Ultimately, McGregor provided an important insight into how enterprises could modernize working conditions, which was a central issue for those studying organizational development* (the study of how large entities such as businesses and institutions develop and evolve).

NOTES

1 Douglas McGregor, *The Human Side of Enterprise* (New York: McGraw-Hill, 1960), 11.

2 McGregor, *Human Side of Enterprise*, 42.

3 McGregor, *Human Side of Enterprise*, 40.

SECTION 2
IDEAS

MODULE 5
MAIN IDEAS

KEY POINTS

- Classical organizational theory, which McGregor called Theory X,* is based on faulty assumptions about human behavior and motivation.
- The reward and punishment system of Theory X is counterproductive.
- McGregor's alternative, which he called Theory Y,* helps managers design working conditions that provide for employee self-esteem, status, and self-actualization.*

Key Themes

In *The Human Side of Enterprise*, Douglas McGregor distinguishes between two different management approaches, which he calls Theory X and Theory Y, showing how each shapes an organization's culture. He hopes to show by this comparison that Theory Y is better for both employees and employers; he also provides a theoretical explanation for how adopting the more humanistic* Theory Y will lead to better outcomes for businesses.

McGregor writes that Theory X is based on incentives: "The practical logic of incentives is that people want money, and that they will work harder to get more of it."[1] According to Theory X, then, people will accept strict controls as long as they are financially rewarded.

However, the book's key point is that this theory is based on a misunderstanding of human nature. The Theory X system fails to create productive, satisfying working conditions, because it does not account for a number of other important factors that influence

> ❝ We can improve our ability to control only if we recognize that control consists in selective adaptation to human nature rather than in attempting to make human nature conform to our wishes. ❞
>
> Douglas McGregor, *The Human Side of Enterprise*

human behavior, assuming instead that people are naturally lazy. As McGregor observes: "Theory X offers management an easy rationalization for ineffective organizational performance: It is due to the nature of the human resources with which we must work."[2]

Exploring the Ideas

McGregor identified three main assumptions about human behavior as held by Theory X.

- "The average human being has an inherent dislike of work and will avoid it if he can."[3]
- "Because of this human characteristic of dislike of work, most people must be coerced, controlled, directed, threatened with punishment to get them to put forth adequate effort toward the achievement of organizational objectives."[4]
- "The average human being prefers to be directed, wishes to avoid responsibility, has relatively little ambition, [and] wants security above all."[5]

If people will only work when coerced and controlled, then they can be managed through a system of rewards and punishments. McGregor calls such a system "the carrot-and-stick motivation" of employees. Under Theory X, employees will only perform work for incentives such as money (the "carrot") and to avoid being disciplined or even fired (the "stick").

The carrot-and-stick system works reasonably well when people are struggling to pay for basic necessities like food and shelter. And indeed, McGregor notes that management can control employees by providing or withholding these needs: "Man tends to live for bread alone when there is little bread."[6]

Additionally, McGregor argues that work itself should be a motivating experience. If the only benefit of work is the creation of wages to be spent outside work, then work begins to look like a form of punishment: something employees only do to make the rest of their lives satisfying. This is problematic, because, as McGregor puts it, companies could "hardly expect them to undergo more of this punishment than is necessary."[7]

For this reason, McGregor believes that work itself should be a satisfying experience: it should bring meaning and self-respect. He proposes an alternative to Theory X that would meet these other, "higher-order," needs. He calls it Theory Y, and its basic assumptions are rooted in the psychological research of the psychologists Abraham Maslow* and Elton Mayo.*

Theory Y's main assumptions are that:

- "[People] will exercise self-direction and self-control in the service of objectives to which [they are] committed."[8]
- "The average human being learns, under proper conditions, not only to accept but to seek responsibility."[9]
- "The capacity to exercise a relatively high degree of imagination, ingenuity, and creativity in the solution of organizational problems is widely, not narrowly, distributed in the population."[10]
- "Under the conditions of modern industrial life, the intellectual potentialities of the average human being are only partially utilized."[11]

Theory Y assumes that employees can grow and develop in the workplace, and that management should explore the potential of human resources, and selectively adapt strategies to individual employees. In addition to the inherent reward of learning new skills at work, Theory Y suggests that employees have needs "that relate to [their] reputation[s]: needs for status, for recognition, for appreciation, for the deserved respect of one's fellows."[12] In this way, Theory Y tries to bring management practices up to date via contemporary notions of human behavior.

Language and Expression

McGregor wanted his theories to make a difference in both the scholarly field of management science, and the real world of management. As such, *The Human Side of Enterprise* was written to inspire both scholars and people in the business community.[13] McGregor was able to draw on his experience as a consultant at a rubber and sealants company to reach an audience outside academia.

McGregor came to be regarded as one of the most significant contributors to the field of organizational development.* Because he wanted his book to be accessible to managers, he included a few chapters that function as a guide to implementing Theory Y in any business enterprise. As a consequence, *The Human Side of Enterprise* has had a massive impact on both business scholars and the business community itself.

NOTES

1   Douglas McGregor, *The Human Side of Enterprise* (New York: McGraw-Hill, 1960), 9.

2   McGregor, *Human Side of Enterprise*, 48.

3   McGregor, *Human Side of Enterprise*, 33.

4   McGregor, *Human Side of Enterprise*, 34.

5   McGregor, *Human Side of Enterprise*, 34.

6   McGregor, *Human Side of Enterprise*, 41.

7   McGregor, *Human Side of Enterprise*, 40.

8   McGregor, *Human Side of Enterprise*, 47.

9   McGregor, *Human Side of Enterprise*, 48.

10 McGregor, *Human Side of Enterprise*, 48.

11 McGregor, *Human Side of Enterprise*, 48.

12 McGregor, *Human Side of Enterprise*, 38.

13 Peter Vaill, "Process Wisdom for a New Age," *ReVISION* 7, no. 2 (1986): 39–49.

MODULE 6
SECONDARY IDEAS

KEY POINTS

- One challenge for McGregor's Theory Y* is that it is difficult to evaluate worker performance: when employees direct themselves, how should wages and salary raises be determined?

- McGregor recommended using the Scanlon Plan,* which was invented by steelworker and local union president Joseph Scanlon* during the 1930s. The Scanlon Plan was based on employee participation and cost-reduction sharing* (in which employees receive a share of the company's profits).

- Theory Y's objectives for managers have not been widely implemented today because companies have not devoted themselves to promoting learning and growth among their workers.

Other Ideas

An important secondary idea in *The Human Side of Enterprise* is Douglas McGregor's exploration of how performance reviews might be changed to reflect the assumptions of Theory Y. According to one scholarly analysis, performance reviews during McGregor's time "were mostly performed in a manner consistent with Theory X. That is, they were unilateral in nature and clearly represented a method of external control by the supervisor, manager and the organization."[1] McGregor suggested that changing how workers were evaluated could positively reshape an entire organization.

McGregor introduced a method of appraisal characterized

> ** A still greater degree of participation would
> be involved if the superior were to present his
> subordinates a problem facing him with the request
> that they help him find the best solution to it. **

Douglas McGregor, *The Human Side of Enterprise*

by a dialogue between different organizational levels, notably between lower and high-ranking managers and their employees, for the purpose of nurturing cooperation. McGregor advocated synchronizing employees' goals with those of the company; he argued that performance reviews should not result in reward or punishment, but, rather, should encourage employees at all levels to participate in improving the company's performance.

Exploring the Ideas

McGregor argued that employees should have more control over their tasks and responsibilities, and that those responsibilities should be aligned with the organization's overall objectives. This method of management was first introduced by management consultant Peter Drucker* in his *The Practice of Management* (1954) and is now commonly known as "management by objectives (MBO)."*

McGregor builds on Drucker's method by focusing on how relationships can be built within an organization. Performance reviews, he believed, should be based on the results of those relationships, and not on an individual's performance alone.[2] This creates an organizational structure that is humanistic,* in that it values the growth and development of individual workers, and also one that draws on the knowledge of those who study behavioral management.

McGregor was also an advocate of the Scanlon Plan, named after the steelworker and unionist Joseph Scanlon (a union is an organization of workers founded to secure better working conditions or pay). The Scanlon Plan[3] is a management philosophy that focuses on cost-reduction sharing and effective participation, consistent with Theory Y principles.

Cost-reduction sharing means, according to McGregor, that employees share in the economic gains "from improvements in organizational performance."[4] They receive a monthly bonus on top of their wages depending on the output of the organization as a whole. This helps them "see the connection between their behavior and organizational achievement"—that is, it allows them to see their personal success as being tied up with the company's overall success.[5]

The other aspect of the Scanlon Plan—effective participation— means establishing committees in which employees meet for brief brainstorming sessions (that is, spontaneously developing, and then discussing, ideas). McGregor notes that, by doing this, the company receives "economically significant ideas" that could save them using the services of an outside consultant. These two principles—cost reduction sharing and effective participation—can also improve relationships between workers on the shop floor (the physical space where employees work).

Overlooked

Since its publication in 1960, *The Human Side of Enterprise* has been thoroughly examined by generations of academics. Businesses, however, have yet to truly adopt management models that promote employee self-actualization*—workers' opportunity to realize their full creative potential.

McGregor argued that if businesses were to promote self-actualization and humanistic values, they would benefit from increased worker satisfaction, which would in turn lead to better results (in terms of efficiency and productivity). It would also lead to a lower job turnover rate, and so reduce the costs of hiring and training new employees. In terms of the culture of the workplace and assumptions regarding the needs of employees, McGregor believed that Theory Y would work as a self-fulfilling prophecy were it to be fully adopted.[6]

Today, however, organizations fall short of "providing opportunities for self-actualization."[7] One reason for this is that employees now tend to change jobs at a much higher rate than when McGregor wrote *The Human Side of Enterprise*; as a result, organizations have come to reconsider how much to invest in employee development—including opportunities for self-actualization.[8]

NOTES

1   Peter Sorensen and Matt Minahan, "McGregor's Legacy: The Evolution and Current Application of Theory Y Management," *Journal of Management History* 17, no. 2 (2011): 178–92.

2   Richard Babcock, "Tracing the History of MBO," in *Strategies and Tactics in Management by Objectives,* ed. Richard Babcock and Peter F. Sorensen (Champaign, IL: Stipes, 1976), 2–24.

3   Business Dictionary, "Scanlon Plan," accessed November 20, 2015, www.businessdictionary.com/definition/scanlon-plan.html.

4   Douglas McGregor, *The Human Side of Enterprise* (New York; McGraw-Hill, 1960), 111.

5   McGregor, *Human Side of Enterprise*, 112.

6   Sorensen and Minahan, "McGregor's Legacy."

7   Thomas C. Head, "Douglas McGregor's Legacy: Lessons Learned, Lessons Lost," *Journal of Management History* 17, no. 2 (2011): 202–16.

8   Rensis Likert, *The Human Organization: Its Management and Value* (New York: McGraw-Hill, 1967).

MODULE 7
ACHIEVEMENT

KEY POINTS

- *The Human Side of Enterprise* began as an article of the same title.[1]

- McGregor cautioned that an environment dominated by Theory X* practices, founded on the assumptions that workers are idle and will operate only under strict control or for monetary incentives, is not conducive to the implementation of Theory Y* practices.

- McGregor acknowledged that applying Theory Y would take time, since many organizations had a long history of using Theory X management strategies.

Assessing the Argument

Although Douglas McGregor's *The Human Side of Enterprise* focuses on the controlling style of Theory X management—in particular, coercion and punishment—he also acknowledges that certain Theory X approaches are more subtle than others. Some managers are permissive, for example, focusing on satisfying employees' demands to achieve harmony in the workplace. Ultimately, McGregor notes, this subtler approach is simply another form of control and just as counterproductive as sterner strategies; it means that employees can expect more and give less effort in return.

McGregor claims that it does not matter what kind of Theory X management style is used, as all lead to the company failing to meet its economic objectives. Theory X practices also fail to create working conditions in which people thrive, since they meet only physiological needs (needs related to food and

> ❝ We tend to think that the boss is a boss is a boss is a boss. This is not the case at all. The circumstances change from hour to hour, and from day to day as the manager undertakes different activities, and the methods of influence which are appropriate shift accordingly. ❞
>
> Douglas McGregor, *The Human Side of Enterprise*

shelter) and safety needs (the desire to work in environments that are not dangerous).

On the other hand, under Theory Y strategy, management can be flexible enough to address its workforce's social needs (needs related to collaboration and sense of belonging) and egoistic needs (which include self-confidence, independence, achievement, knowledge, appreciation, status, and recognition). After that, organizations can work to fulfill their employees' self-actualization* needs.[2]

For McGregor, it was more important that management abandon its limiting assumptions about people, such as those identified in his Theory X, than that they accept the assumptions of Theory Y.[3] He did, however, hope that managers would develop their practices to account for the varied needs of their workers. So Theory Y was important insofar as it was a proposed replacement for Theory X, but McGregor did not see it as the only way forward.

Achievement in Context

McGregor first presented his theory that classical management theories were based on false assumptions about human behavior to the very managers he was studying, and was glad to learn that "an increasing number of managers recognize the inadequacy of present methods."[4] He then shared the research with his colleagues at the School of Industrial Management at MIT.

In this way, McGregor was able to receive feedback about his ideas from both his research subjects and his colleagues; the feedback informed an article, also titled "The Human Side of Enterprise," which he published in 1957. His Theories X and Y sparked a dialogue within the community of management scholars that encouraged him to refine his ideas, eventually presenting them in their most fully developed forms in *The Human Side of Enterprise.*

When his work was first published, managers were receptive to a shift from Theory X to Theory Y objectives. McGregor's argument that businesses would be unable to increase their productivity and efficiency unless they could satisfy workers' needs, as described in Maslow's hierarchy,* was made successfully.

McGregor's Theory X and Theory Y led to substantial research on psychology and management within the field of organizational development.* Moreover, his ideas have been adopted by and have influenced a number of other academic disciplines, among them organizational behavior, leadership, strategy, and human resource management (the management of workers, skills, employment policy, and so on).

Limitations

McGregor himself was the first to acknowledge the limitations of Theory Y, writing: "Theoretical assumptions such as those of Theory Y imply some conditions which are unrealizable in practice."[5] He did not see this as a "handicap," however, but as a stimulus to invention and discovery."[6]

McGregor also realized that some organizations would find it easier to adopt the assumptions of Theory Y than others. It is difficult, if not impossible, for organizations with a long history of Theory X practices to make the transition: major changes in management styles require a complete overhaul in terms of structure, functions, and the sort of people employed as managers.

That said, McGregor does offer a detailed account of how businesses might adopt Theory Y within a short amount of time. He provides an in-depth analysis of organizational theories in order to spark discussion among scholars and the business community; his work advocates collaboration in the area of human resources in industry.[7]

NOTES

1   Douglas McGregor, "The Human Side of Enterprise," first published in *Adventure in Thought and Action*, Proceedings of the Fifth Anniversary Convocation of the School of Industrial Management, Massachusetts Institute of Technology, Cambridge, April 9, 1957 (Cambridge, MA: MIT School of Industrial Management, 1957); reprinted in *The Management Review* 46 (1957): 22–8.

2   Douglas McGregor, *The Human Side of Enterprise* (New York: McGraw-Hill, 1960), 38.

3   McGregor, *Human Side of Enterprise*, 245.

4   McGregor, *Human Side of Enterprise*, 245.

5   McGregor, *Human Side of Enterprise*, 245.

6   McGregor, *Human Side of Enterprise*, 246.

7   McGregor, *Human Side of Enterprise*, 246.

MODULE 8
PLACE IN THE AUTHOR'S WORK

KEY POINTS

- McGregor devoted his career to analyzing the relationship between management styles and worker efficiency. *The Human Side of Enterprise* was his most influential academic work.

- He linked Theory X* practices to a lack of innovation and efficiency.

- McGregor's publications were significant throughout the twentieth century.

Positioning

Douglas McGregor's *The Human Side of Enterprise* offers the insights gleaned from a career spent analyzing management styles; he focused on the importance of staff–line* relationships (the relationships between managers and those they manage) as having the greatest influence on working conditions. McGregor was a staunch humanist,* and believed that workers should be valued as people and given the opportunity to grow.

According to the organizational theorists Daniel Katz* and Robert Kahn,* McGregor's Theory Y* uses "referent power"*— influence based on liking or identification with another person.[1] McGregor advocated collaboration and participation between employees and managers, believing this would strengthen their relationships; Katz and Kahn believed that organizations would be more effective if all their members were able to collaborate and participate with their coworkers.[2]

McGregor touted Theory Y as the management style that

> **❝** The purpose of this volume is not to entice management to choose sides over Theory X or Theory Y. It is, rather, to encourage the realization that theory is important, to urge management to examine its assumptions and make them explicit. In doing so, it will open a door to the future. **❞**
>
> Douglas McGregor, *The Human Side of Enterprise*

would generate the greatest employee satisfaction and the highest productivity. According to Peter Senge,* a management theorist and senior lecturer at MIT, McGregor shows why it is difficult for companies governed by Theory X to innovate—but Theory Y does not necessarily guarantee innovation either.[3]

Unfortunately, McGregor did not have the opportunity to address concerns such as those of Senge; he died only four years after *The Human Side of Enterprise* was published.

Integration

While criticizing management under Theory X, McGregor pointed out that contemporary management practices had "significantly reduced economic hardships, eliminated the more extreme forms of industrial warfare, provided a generally safe and pleasant working environment, but it has done all these things without changing its fundamental theory of management."[4] That is: while Theory X management had satisfied basic needs, it had not gone far enough to change working conditions. Productivity could still improve if organizations changed their assumptions about how employees should be treated.

But not everyone agreed with McGregor's assessment. His claims were based on the psychological dynamics that occur in relationships between managers and their subordinates. Critics therefore argued that McGregor did not account for environmental factors such as the culture in which the business was located, or the economic and legal consequences of government regulation. They argued that these could also affect organizations and reduce efficiency.[5]

A number of companies also rejected McGregor's suggestion that high-ranked officials carried the greatest responsibility for stagnant productivity.

Significance

McGregor anticipated the intellectual needs and movements of his time. When his theories were introduced, they helped modernize the ways in which businesses were structured and managed. His work is important because it combines psychological and managerial concepts, and, in so doing, encourages managers to self-reflect, and to see their workers more humanistically.

In general, McGregor's work has been positively received in organizational management, and he is often referenced in management textbooks. In fact, according to a poll conducted by the *Economist* in 1993, McGregor is the most popular management scholar of all time.[6]

The Human Side of Enterprise itself has also been popular, having been voted the fourth most significant management text of the twentieth century by the Academy of Management, publisher of the highly respected *Academy of Management Journal*. The book was listed in the "25 Most Influential Business Management Books" by *Time* magazine in 2011.[7]

NOTES

1   Daniel Katz and Robert L. Kahn, *The Social Psychology of Organizations* (New York: John Wiley & Sons, 1966), 302.

2   Katz and Kahn, *Social Psychology of Organizations*, 303.

3   Peter M. Senge, "The Practice of Innovation," *Leader to Leader* 9 (1998): 16–22.

4   Douglas McGregor, *The Human Side of Enterprise* (New York: McGraw-Hill, 1960), 46.

5   Warren Bennis, "Chairman Mac in Perspective," *Journal of Management History* 17, no. 2 (2011): 1–11.

6   Tim Hindle, *Guide to Management Ideas and Gurus* (London: Profile Books, 2008).

7   "The 25 Most Influential Business Management Books," *Time*, accessed November 20, 2015, http://content.time.com/time/specials/packages/completelist/0,29569,2086680,00.html.

SECTION 3
IMPACT

MODULE 9
THE FIRST RESPONSES

KEY POINTS

- *The Human Side of Enterprise* attracted a great deal of scholarly attention when it was first published in 1960.
- McGregor was criticized by those who favored traditional management styles.
- Some argued that McGregor's Theory Y* misrepresented human nature.

Criticism

Douglas McGregor's critique of Theory X* in *The Human Side of Enterprise* was itself criticized by those who favored traditional management techniques. They accused McGregor of having a "distorted" idea of human nature.[1] In particular, they believed that human beings behave differently in different settings; workplace behavior is not the same as family or community behavior.

Additionally, McGregor's humanistic* values provoked criticism, even though his tone had been moderate and objective. And while the influential psychologist Abraham Maslow's* hierarchy of needs* provided a firm foundation for Theory Y, the theory had its limits—which meant that McGregor's work likewise had limits. In fact, Maslow himself was one of McGregor's critics; he believed that Theory Y was too idealistic and impractical to apply to workplaces.[2]

Other critics, such as McGregor's colleague at MIT, Edgar Schein,* agreed with Maslow;[3] for Schein, while Theory Y's assumptions about human nature are realistic, management does not have a responsibility to include employees in the decision-making

> **66** ... authority is an inappropriate method of control on which to place exclusive reliance in United States industry today ... under certain circumstances it may be essential, but for promoting collaboration it is at best a weak crutch. **99**
>
> Douglas McGregor, *The Human Side of Enterprise*

process.[4] As such, he believed that Theory Y should only be applied to those in upper management positions.[5]

McGregor was also criticized for the way he obtained and interpreted data. One scholar observed: "McGregor based his arguments in part on impressionistic observation and practiced hypothesis testing only in a casual manner."[6] In other words, McGregor was so focused on improving employees' working conditions that he may have overlooked some of the challenges of implementing Theory Y.

Responses

Other responses were more nuanced. For example, Geert Hofstede,* the prominent Dutch cross-cultural psychologist* (a psychologist who examines psychological differences and similarities across cultural borders) suggested that both Theory X and Theory Y were based on overly broad assumptions about human nature. In particular, Hofstede argued that they do not take into account how uncertainty avoidance*—the degree to which people are willing to accept the unexpected—varies from culture to culture.

According to Hofstede, there are some countries in which people are less prepared to cope with uncertainty and should therefore have less influence on decision-making. In those situations, Theory X might work better than Theory Y. In the light of this, it seems unreasonable to advocate a total abandonment of Theory X practices.[7]

McGregor's work also served as a foundation for other academics, such as the management scholar William Ouchi,* who proposed Theory Z* in 1981.[8] Ouchi wanted to provide American companies with a competitive edge by implementing some of the characteristics of Japanese business corporations, which had been highly successful in the 1970s. At that time, Japanese companies provided lifelong employment and focused on employee well-being. This led to high employee morale and economic success.[9]

Conflict and Consensus

Among the challenges to his work, McGregor was particularly compelled to respond to Hofstede's critique that the culture in which an organization exists affects the effectiveness of Theory X or Theory Y. Hofstede urged McGregor to provide more details about which environments his theories were most applicable to.[10]

McGregor's colleague Edgar Schein initially defended McGregor by noting that Theory X and Theory Y are simply labels that describe two different sets of beliefs that managers seem to hold about their workers. McGregor did not demand that all organizations adopt Theory Y practices—he merely proposed Theory Y as a possible alternative to Theory X. In the introduction to McGregor's 1967 *The Professional Manager* (published after his death), Schein wrote that "few readers were willing to acknowledge that the content of Doug's book made such a neutral point."[11]

Those who later used McGregor's work were careful to adjust his ideas to account for the way in which culture influences work environments.

NOTES

1   Harold Guetzkow, review of *Leadership and Organization: A Behavioral Science Approach* by Robert Tannenbaum, Irving R. Weschler, and Fred Massarik, *American Sociological Review* 26, no. 5 (1961): 804.

2   Abraham H. Maslow, *Eupsychian Management: A Journal* (Homewood, IL: Irwin, 1965).

3   Edgar Schein, "In Defense of Theory Y," *Organizational Dynamics* 4 (1975): 17–30.

4   Edgar Schein, "Relationships between Sex Role Stereotypes and Requisite Management Characteristics among Female Managers," *Journal of Applied Psychology* 60, no. 3 (1975): 340–4.

5   David Jacobs, "Book Review Essay: Douglas McGregor: The Human Side of Enterprise in Peril," *Academy of Management Review* 29, no. 2 (2004): 293–6.

6   Jacobs, "Book Review," 294.

7   Carol M. Sanchez and Dawn M. Curtis, "Different Minds and Common Problems: Geert Hofstede's Research on National Cultures," *Performance Improvement Quarterly* 13, no. 2 (2000): 9–19.

8   William G. Ouchi, *Theory Z: How American Business Can Meet the Japanese Challenge* (Reading, MA: Addison-Wesley, 1981).

9   Mind Tools Editorial Team, "Theory Z: Merging Eastern and Western Management Styles," accessed November 24, 2015, www.mindtools.com/pages/article/theory-z.htm.

10 Warren Bennis, "Chairman Mac in Perspective," *Journal of Management History* 17, no. 2 (2011): 1–11.

11 Douglas McGregor, *The Professional Manager* (New York: McGraw-Hill, 1967), 11.

KEY POINTS

- McGregor successfully convinced many managers to adopt Theory Y* principles.

- Some of McGregor's ideas were used in combination with contingency theories* (theories about how management and leadership practices should adapt or change to match a market or culture).

- Those who built on McGregor's work identified specific circumstances and cultural contexts in which either Theory X* or Theory Y would be more applicable.

Uses and Problems

Douglas McGregor's theories, as discussed in his *The Human Side of Enterprise*, were speedily introduced into companies because they promised growth and increased efficiency. At the multinational consumer goods company Proctor and Gamble, for example, executives applied Theory Y to one of their manufacturing plants. They attempted to implement a management structure in which employees all held similar ranks, decision-making was determined by management by objectives ("MBO,"* according to which employees developed detailed plans to achieve company goals),[1] and in which performance was regularly monitored.[2] Ultimately, the plant increased its productivity by 30 percent.[3]

Managers generally accepted McGregor's proposal that applying Abraham Maslow's* hierarchy of needs* to the workplace would both improve employee collaboration and communication, and motivate workers to grow and learn. McGregor was not quite as

> **66** At times he [the manager] may be in the role
> of the leader of a group of subordinates; at other
> times he may be a member of a group of his peers.
> Sometimes he is in the role of teacher; at other
> times he may be a decision maker, a disciplinarian, a
> helper, a consultant, or simply an observer. **99**
>
> Douglas McGregor, *The Human Side of Enterprise*

successful within the scholarly community following the psychologist
Geert Hofstede's* criticism that the success of Theory X or Theory
Y depends on cultural context. That said, scholars still built upon the
theories and ideas presented in *The Human Side of Enterprise.*

Schools of Thought

Scholars further explored the ways in which the implementation
of Theories X and Y affect how organizations adapt and learn. For
example, based on McGregor's work, the management theorist Peter
Senge* coined the term "learning organization,"* which refers to
companies that are able to transform themselves by encouraging
their employees to learn.

Learning organizations are based on the idea that there is no best
way to manage; instead, the best managers are able to adapt to new
situations and to account for changing market environments. In
other words, a strategy effective in one situation may be ineffective
in another. This is also sometimes called contingency theory; today,
a great deal of evidence exists to support it.[4]

In Current Scholarship

Today, scholars who draw on *The Human Side of Enterprise* take
into account Hofstede's warnings about how Theories X and Y are
affected by culture. This has opened new directions for research.

For example, the British professor of organization sociology Joan Woodward[*] argues that while Theory X is applicable to enterprises engaged in mass production, Theory Y is more relevant to those making complex, advanced products.[5] Edgar Schein,[*] McGregor's colleague at MIT, proposed a new version of Theory Y that was based not on humanistic[*] principles, but on those of contingency theory.[6]

Other scholars have argued that Theory X works in stable environments, and Theory Y in rapidly changing environments.[7] Still others suggest that various theories can be used in different departments of the same organization: managers can create varied working conditions depending on their beliefs and the culture of the department itself.[8]

Generally speaking, scholars have shifted their attention away from classifying management styles as X or Y, and from promoting humanistic values within organizations.[9]

NOTES

1   Richard Babcock, "Tracing the History of MBO," in *Strategies and Tactics in Management by Objectives*, ed. Richard Babcock and Peter F. Sorensen (Champaign, IL: Stipes, 1976): 2–24.

2   "Management by Objectives," *Economist*, accessed November 20, 2015, www.economist.com/node/14299761.

3   Robert Waterman, *The Frontiers of Excellence: Learning from Companies That Put People First* (London: Nicholas Brealey Publishing, 1994).

4   David Jacobs, "Book Review Essay: Douglas McGregor: The Human Side of Enterprise in Peril," *Academy of Management Review* 29, no. 2 (2004): 293–6.

5   Joan Woodward, *Industrial Organization: Theory and Practice* (New York: Oxford University Press, 1965).

6   Edgar Schein, "Relationships between Sex Role Stereotypes and Requisite Management Characteristics among Female Managers," *Journal of Applied Psychology* 60, no. 3 (1975): 340–4.

7   Tom Burns and George M. Stalker, *The Management of Innovations* (London: Tavistock, 1961).

8   Paul R. Lawrence and Jay William Lorsch, "High Performing Organizations in Three Environments," in *Organization and Environment: Managing Differentiation and Integration*, ed. Paul R. Lawrence and Jay William Lorsch (Boston, MA: Harvard Business School, 1967), 133–58.

9   Don Hellriegel, Susan E. Jackson, and John W. Slocum, *Management: A Competency-Based Approach* (Cincinnati, OH: South-Western Publishing, 2002).

MODULE 11
IMPACT AND INFLUENCE TODAY

KEY POINTS

- McGregor wanted to change how employees were evaluated.

- Scholars advocate that organizations become "learning organizations,"* defined by their ability to adapt to changing circumstances.

- McGregor continues to influence the conversation within the academic field of management.

Position

In *The Human Side of Enterprise*, Douglas McGregor linked a company's ability to innovate with its managers' ability to assess their own management styles, believing it important that they reflect on the ways in which their specific styles affect their employees.

Similarly, he argued that employees should be provided with objective feedback, and that managers should not conduct annual performance reviews. The problem with such reviews, he wrote, was that they "provided 'feedback' about behavior at a time remote from the behavior itself."[1] He also believed that individuals should not receive merit pay, since it is based on a manager's subjective opinion.

Instead, McGregor proposed group rewards that were based on objective measures of the group's performance. The most outstanding performers within a group would also be given a substantial bonus. However, individual merit pay, and not group pay, is still commonly awarded in American businesses.

A number of scholars continue to develop McGregor's work today. The management scholar Peter Senge* has elaborated on

> **❝ With every passing year, McGregor's message becomes ever more relevant, timelier and more important. ❞**
>
> Peter Drucker, in Sultan Kermally's *Gurus on People Management*

McGregor's ideas as to why it is important for managers to reflect on how their practices affect staff–line (or manager–subordinate) relationships.*[2] He has suggested that it is difficult for managers to notice their own assumptions about people if they are constantly focused on achieving goals.[3] And the American business theorist Chris Argyris* suggested that organizations that aspire to be learning organizations should create working conditions that encourage innovation, creativity, and efficiency.[4]

Interaction

Organizational behaviorists*—those who investigate the workings of organizations, on the basis that behavior offers important insight into human psychology—have supported McGregor's view that intense control mechanisms can cause employees to become submissive, and that this is ultimately bad for companies. An organization's leadership should use its power to create mutually beneficial relationships between managers and employees.

Following Geert Hofstede's* criticism that McGregor's Theory Y* does not account for cultural differences, scholars have erased the strict borders between Theories X* and Y. This means that discussions between proponents of each school have shifted away from defining types of management in these terms. Instead, newer "contingency theories"* combine elements of both. In this way, today's theories of management still incorporate McGregor's work.

One scholar recently acknowledged the value of *The Human Side of Enterprise* for the field of organizational management,* but also criticized it for focusing so much on the psychological relationship between managers and their employees, and perhaps for overlooking the culture of the entire organization.[5]

The Continuing Debate

Nearly five decades after McGregor published *The Human Side of Enterprise,* his work continues to influence scholarly literature about organizational development.*[6] His influence on the field is most obvious when we examine how often he is referred to in the work of other scholars.

McGregor was integral to scholarship throughout the 1980s. In 2000, *Douglas McGregor, Revisited: Managing the Human Side of the Enterprise,* sparked new interest in his scholarship. The book contains excerpts of his work and is optimistic that, in the future, we can live in "a world of work that we could call "McGregorian.""[7]

In 2004, McGregor was praised for encouraging increased employee participation in the workplace. As one reviewer put it, "McGregor's moral outlook … reflects [his] awareness of the consequences of management choice for workers."[8] In 2011, the *Journal of Management History* devoted an entire issue, with contributions from different academics, to McGregor's legacy, contributions, and limitations.[9] A well-known management scholar wrote that McGregor has left "a lasting impression" on the world of business and management studies.[10]

It is clear, then, that McGregor's work remains relevant to today's discussion.

NOTES

1   Douglas McGregor, *The Human Side of Enterprise* (New York: McGraw-Hill, 1960), 87.

2   Peter Senge, "The Practice of Innovation," *Leader to Leader* 9 (1998): 16–22.

3   Peter Senge, *The Fifth Discipline: The Art and Practice of the Learning Organization* (New York: Doubleday, 1990).

4   Chris Argyris, *Teaching Smart People How to Learn* (Boston, MA: Harvard Business Press, 1998).

5   Warren Bennis, "Chairman Mac in Perspective," *Journal of Management History* 17, no. 2 (2011): 1–11.

6   W. Warren Burke, *Organization Change: Theory and Practice* (Thousand Oaks, CA: Sage, 2008); W. Warren Burke, "The Douglas McGregor Legacy," *Journal of Applied Behavioral Science* 45 (2009): 8–11.

7   Gary Heil, Warren Bennis, and Deborah C. Stephens, *Douglas McGregor, Revisited: Managing the Human Side of the Enterprise* (New York: Wiley, 2000), viii.

8   David Jacobs, "Book Review Essay: Douglas McGregor: The Human Side of Enterprise in Peril," *Academy of Management Review* 29, no. 2 (2004): 293–6.

9   Peter F. Sorensen and Matt Minahan, "McGregor's Legacy: The Evolution and Current Application of Theory Y Management," *Journal of Management History* 17, no. 2 (2011): 178–92.

10 Robert A. Cunningham, "Douglas McGregor: A Lasting Impression," *Ivey Business Journal* 75 (2011): 5–7.

MODULE 12
WHERE NEXT?

KEY POINTS

- One reason McGregor's Theory Y* has not been widely implemented today is that companies tend to engage in short-term planning, which inhibits them from investing in employees' long-term growth.

- McGregor's *The Human Side of Enterprise* is valuable when interpreting current economic trends, such as the recent recession in the United States.

- Management under Theory X* may lead to offices that resemble "electronic sweatshops."*

Potential

As much as Douglas McGregor's *The Human Side of Enterprise* encouraged companies to invest in their employees' personal growth, today most companies engage in strategic planning that covers no more than the next three years of business.[1] This has created instability in the employment market, since companies do not plan for their employees' long-term futures; it also encourages human resource managers to hire employees who are already trained, rather than to spend time developing an untrained employee.[2]

One reason for this is that it is costly to invest in workers at a time when so many people change jobs frequently; these costs tend to offset the higher productivity that McGregor argued would result from Theory Y practices. That said, managers continue to draw on Theory Y assumptions to encourage creativity and innovation.

The criticism that McGregor's work did not account for cultural differences is also still valid today. Twenty-first century companies

> **66** ...his moral perspective on human relations remains valuable even in altered circumstances. In fact, in this era of downsizing, pension insecurity, and aggressive investors seeking immediate return, it is useful to reconsider McGregor's call to honor the unfulfilled potential of employees. **99**
>
> David Jacobs, *Book Review Essay: Douglas McGregor: The Human Side of Enterprise in Peril*

have diverse workforces: their employees and managers come from a wide range of places and cultures. This means that organizations may differ from department to department, and varying styles of management may be effective for different employees.

It is exactly this aspect of McGregor's work that would benefit from further development. Adapting his theories for a multicultural context would update them for businesses today.

Future Directions

The recent economic recession in the United States, dubbed the "Great Recession,"* illustrates the significance of McGregor's work. This period of economic downturn (2007–9) was characterized by higher unemployment (from 5 percent in 2007 to 10 percent in 2009), low wages, temporary employment, and deteriorating working conditions, including the loss of fringe benefits such as health insurance.[3] Millions of Americans struggled to find jobs that would pay the bills and provide for their families. This brings to mind McGregor's observation that "the individual can be controlled so long as he is struggling for subsistence. Man tends to live for bread alone when there is little bread."[4] High unemployment provided management with an opportunity to focus on economic objectives, and in the process to ignore workers' job satisfaction.

As a result, many companies today follow Theory X assumptions and principles; furthermore, they can now use technology that fits a Theory X approach, such as computer surveillance that allows them to monitor employees at all times. In modern call centers, for example, pop-ups may appear on employees' computer screens telling them they need to work faster. This has led some scholars to argue that these technologies transform offices into "electronic sweatshops."[5]

Summary

In *The Human Side of Enterprise,* Douglas McGregor contrasts two opposing types of management. Under Theory X, managers assume that employees want to do as little work as possible, and that a system of strict control and rewards is needed. In contrast, Theory Y management recognizes that employees need growth, learning, responsibility, and creativity to be good workers. McGregor is in favor of Theory Y, arguing that it increases efficiency and productivity.

The research of McGregor and his successors ultimately led to a new way of thinking about how organizations should behave: contingency theory,* which calls for management to adapt an organization's needs and economic aims to the economy and culture of the society in which it exists. Companies should become "learning organizations"* through the application of Theory Y principles, so that they can adapt to new, changing, and dynamic markets.

We can see, then, that even though McGregor died in 1964, his work continues to influence both businesses and those who study them.

NOTES

1   Thomas C. Head, "Douglas McGregor's Legacy: Lessons Learned, Lessons Lost," *Journal of Management History* 17, no. 2 (2011): 202–16.

2   William P. Anthony, K. Michele Kacmar and Pamela L. Perrewe, *Human Resource Management: A Strategic Approach* (Mason, OH: Thomson/ South-Western, 2006).

3   Monica Kirkpatrick Johnson, Rayna Amber Sage, and Jeylan T. Mortimer, "Work Values, Early Career Difficulties, and the U.S. Economic Recession," *Social Psychology Quarterly* 75, no. 3 (2012): 242–67.

4   Douglas McGregor, *The Human Side of Enterprise* (New York: McGraw-Hill, 1960), 41.

5   Paul Attewell, "Big Brother and the Sweatshop: Computer Surveillance in the Automated Office," *Sociological Theory* 5 (1987): 87–100.

GLOSSARIES

GLOSSARY OF TERMS

Alfred P. Sloan Foundation: a not-for-profit organization. It was founded in 1934 by Alfred Pritchard Sloan Jr., who spent his career as an executive at the automobile company General Motors. Sloan's purpose for his foundation was to provide grants for innovative research in science and technology.

Behavioral management: a type of management that emphasizes the human dimension of work. It views human beings as individual resources who have potential for growth. It is also known as the human relations movement.

Behaviorism: the theory that human behavior offers important insights into human psychology, and that it can be measured, trained, and changed.

Contingency theory: a management theory based on the belief that decisions and leadership are dependent upon the environment in which the organization operates.

Cost-reduction sharing: a policy in which employees share the financial rewards of an organization's success (increased productivity or decreased production costs, for example). Employees receive monthly bonuses on top of their basic wages.

Cross-cultural psychology: a branch of psychology that examines psychological differences and similarities across cultural borders.

Electronic sweatshops: places of work in which employees are constantly monitored by the management using computer surveillance. "Sweatshop" itself is a term for a business in which employees are exploited and have to work long hours for little pay.

Great Depression: the decade following the 1929 stock market crash, during which millions of Americans could not find work and lived in poverty.

Great Recession: the collapse of the financial markets in the United States between 2007 and 2009 that left millions of Americans unemployed. At the height of the Great Recession, the unemployment rate was nearly 10 percent.

Group dynamics: the study of how humans behave in groups. First coined by the psychologist Kurt Lewin.

Hierarchy of needs: a concept developed by the psychologist Abraham Maslow to describe and rank different types of human motivation. The pyramid of needs that he identified ranged from basic physiological needs (the need for food and shelter), through to the need for fulfillment and self-actualization.

Humanism: a philosophy that holds that individual human beings should have the opportunity to realize their full potential. From a business perspective, humanistic working conditions combine both employees' needs and the company's goals in order to achieve higher efficiency.

Learning organization: a learning organization is rooted in the idea that there is no best form of management. Such an organization has the flexibility to adapt to its environment (economic and cultural) through a shared vision of all employees, and a focus on team learning.

Management by Objectives (MBO): a system whereby managers and employees collaborate to develop objectives and plans. These plans are regularly monitored to ensure that they remain on track.

McGregor Institute: a charitable organization dedicated to helping people who are struggling to find work. It was founded in 1895 by Douglas McGregor's grandfather.

Organizational behaviorists: those engaged in the systemic study of the function of organizations, using behaviorist assumptions and methods.

Organizational development (OD): an academic field focused on understanding and managing organizational change. Kurt Lewin is generally seen as the father of organizational development.

Organizational psychology: the systematic study of how the workplace affects the human mind.

Natural soldiering: the tendency of workers to take it easy while working.

Postwar period: the period of adjustment after World War II, when millions of soldiers returned to the United States, and Europe had to rebuild itself.

Psychoanalysis: a therapeutic method and theoretical approach to the behavioral phenomena and conditions provoked by unconscious thought.

Referent power: a term coined by management scholars Daniel Katz and Robert Kahn to describe the power that managers obtain from being liked by their subordinates.

Scanlon Plan: a plan developed by the unionist and steelworker Joseph Scanlon in the 1930s to help businesses cope with the economic climate. The plan called for businesses to draw on the potential of their employees, and for employee collaboration.

Scientific management: the idea that organizations can be managed on the basis of scientific principles. It is also known as "Taylorism" after the industrialist and early management scholar Frederick Winslow Taylor.

Self-actualization: the fulfillment of an individual's creative potential.

Self-initiative: the ability of employees to start work without being told by managers what to do.

Staff–line relationships: a term describing the relationship between superiors (staff) and their employees/subordinates (line). Originally referred to managers and employees working in an assembly-line setting.

Systematic soldiering: the idea that when one or more employees perform the absolute minimum required by their job, other employees will also begin to do as little as possible.

Theory X: a management theory based on the assumption that people are idle and will operate only under strict control or for monetary incentives. Describes traditional management principles, based on Sigmund Freud's psychoanalysis and F. W. Taylor's scientific management principles.

Theory Y: a management theory that assumes people are self-motivated and do not need to be strictly controlled. Under Theory Y's assumptions, employees want to work hard in order to learn and grow.

Theory Z: a theory developed by William G. Ouchi based on the success of Japanese businesses. It suggests that American businesses should draw on Eastern management styles, which value (among other things) employee well-being.

Uncertainty avoidance: the degree to which people in a given country or culture accept unexpected situations, uncertainty, and ambiguity. The notion of uncertainty avoidance was developed by the Dutch cross-cultural psychologist Geert Hofstede.

PEOPLE MENTIONED IN THE TEXT

Theodore M. Alfred (1925–2007) was a professor of management policy at Case Western Reserve University in Cleveland, Ohio; he received a PhD in Industrial Economics from the Massachusetts Institute of Technology (MIT), where he collaborated with Douglas McGregor.

Chris Argyris (1923–2013) was an American business theorist and professor at Harvard Business School who focused on behavior in organizations.

Alex Bavelas (b. 1920) is an American psychologist and professor of business management at the Massachusetts Institute of Technology (MIT), where he started a group networks laboratory.

Peter Drucker (1909–2005) was an Austrian-born American lecturer and management consultant. His books included *Concept of the Corporation* (1972) and *Management: Tasks, Responsibilities, and Practices* (1974).

Mary Parker Follett (1868–1933) was a social worker who later became a management theorist. She is seen as a pioneer in organizational theory and organizational behavior.

Sigmund Freud (1856–1939) was an Austrian neurologist. He is famed for founding psychoanalysis, a therapeutic and theoretical model for the treatment of psychological disorders by addressing patients' unconscious conflicts.

Geert Hofstede (b. 1928) is a Dutch social psychologist who focuses on cross-cultural groups and organizations. He is well known for developing the cultural dimensions theory.

Robert L. Kahn (b. 1918) is an American psychologist who specializes in organizational theory and survey research. He coauthored *The Social Psychology of Organizations* with Daniel Katz, which was published in 1966.

Daniel Katz (1903–98) was an American psychologist and an expert in organizational psychology. He was a professor at the University of Michigan and is best known for his 1966 book, *The Social Psychology of Organizations*.

Anthony Lerner is an external organization development consultant and a principal at Arthur Lerner Associates.

Kurt Lewin (1890–1947) was a pioneering German American psychologist in the fields of social and organizational psychology. He contributed research on group dynamics and organizational development.

Abraham Maslow (1908–70) was an American psychologist who developed what became known as Maslow's hierarchy of needs.

Elton Mayo (1880–1949) was an Australian psychologist, organizational theorist, and industrial researcher who studied the behavior of people in groups.

William G. Ouchi (b. 1943) is a professor of management and organizations at the University of California Los Angeles' Anderson School of Management. He is well known for his book *Theory Z* (1981), in which he proposes that a combination of Eastern and Western styles of management would benefit American business corporations.

Joseph Scanlon (1899–1956) was a steelworker and local union president who invented the Scanlon Plan, which was based on cost-reduction sharing and employee participation. He was invited by Douglas McGregor to become a lecturer at the Massachusetts Institute for Technology.

Edgar Schein (b. 1928) is a former professor at the Massachusetts Institute of Technology, a colleague of Douglas McGregor, and a social psychologist who published work about corporate culture.

Peter Senge (b. 1947) is a management theorist and senior lecturer at the Massachusetts Institute of Technology's School of Management. He founded the Society for Organizational Learning.

B. F. Skinner (1904–90) was an American psychologist and behaviorist who taught at Harvard University. He is generally seen as a key figure in the development of modern behaviorism.

Alfred P. Sloan (1875–1966) was a wealthy automotive business executive who established the School of Industrial Management at the Massachusetts Institute of Technology in 1952.

Frederick Winslow Taylor (1856–1915) was an engineer who is credited with developing the theory and practice of scientific management, which became the basis for classical organizational theory.

John B. Watson (1878–1958) was an American psychologist who founded the psychological school of behaviorism.

Joan Woodward (1916–71) was a British professor in organization sociology at Imperial College London.

WORKS CITED

WORKS CITED

Anthony, William P., K. Michele Kacmar, and Pamela L. Perrewe. *Human Resource Management: A Strategic Approach*. Mason, OH: Thomson/South-Western, 2006.

Argyris, Chris. *Teaching Smart People How to Learn*. Boston, MA: Harvard Business Press, 1998.

Attewell, Paul. "Big Brother and the Sweatshop: Computer Surveillance in the Automated Office." *Sociological Theory* 5 (1987): 87–100.

Babcock, Richard. "Tracing the History of MBO." In *Strategies and Tactics in Management by Objectives,* edited by Richard Babcock and Peter F. Sorensen, 2–24. Champaign, IL: Stipes, 1976.

Bennis, Warren. "Chairman Mac in Perspective." *Journal of Management History* 17, no. 2 (2011): 1–11.

Burke, W. Warren. "The Douglas McGregor Legacy." *Journal of Applied Behavioral Science* 45 (2009): 8–11.

———. *Organization Change: Theory and Practice*. Thousand Oaks, CA: Sage, 2008.

Burns, Tom, and George M. Stalker. *The Management of Innovation*. London: Tavistock, 1961.

Business Dictionary. "Scanlon Plan." Accessed November 20, 2015. www.businessdictionary.com/definition/scanlon-plan.html.

Cunningham, Robert A. "Douglas McGregor: A Lasting Impression." *Ivey Business Journal* 75 (2011): 5–7.

Freud, Sigmund. "An Outline of Psycho-analysis." *International Journal of Psychoanalysis* 21 (1940): 27–84.

Guetzkow, Harold. Review of *Leadership and Organization: A Behavioral Science Approach* by Robert Tannenbaum, Irving R. Weschler, and Fred Massarik. *American Sociological Review* 26, no. 5 (1961): 804.

Head, Thomas C. "Douglas McGregor's Legacy: Lessons Learned, Lessons Lost." *Journal of Management History* 17, no. 2 (2011): 202–16.

Heil, Gary, Warren Bennis, and Deborah C. Stephens. *Douglas McGregor, Revisited: Managing the Human Side of the Enterprise*. New York: Wiley, 2000.

Hellriegel, Don, Susan E. Jackson, and John W. Slocum. *Management: A Competency-Based Approach*. Cincinnati, OH: South-Western Publishing, 2002.

Hindle, Tim. *Guide to Management Ideas and Gurus.* London: Profile Books, 2008.

Jacobs, David. "Book Review Essay: Douglas McGregor: The Human Side of Enterprise in Peril." *Academy of Management Review* 29, no. 2 (2004): 293–6.

Johnson, Monica Kirkpatrick, Rayna Amber Sage, and Jeylan T. Mortimer. "Work Values, Early Career Difficulties, and the U.S. Economic Recession." *Social Psychology Quarterly* 75, no. 3 (2012): 242–67.

Katz, Daniel, and Robert L. Kahn. *The Social Psychology of Organizations*. New York: John Wiley & Sons, 1966.

Kermally, Sultan. *Gurus on People Management.* London: Thorogood, 2004.

Lawrence, Paul R., and Jay William Lorsch. "High Performing Organizations in Three Environments." In *Organization and Environment: Managing Differentiation and Integration*, edited by Paul R. Lawrence and Jay William Lorsch, 133–58. Boston, MA: Harvard Business School, 1967.

Lerner, Arthur. "McGregor's Legacy: Thoughts on What He Left, What Transpired, and What Remains to Pursue." *Journal of Management History* 17, no. 2 (2011): 217–37.

Likert, Rensis. *The Human Organization: Its Management and Value.* New York: McGraw-Hill, 1967.

"Management by Objectives." *Economist*, Accessed November 20, 2015. www.economist.com/node/14299761.

Managers-Net. "Douglas McGregor." Accessed November 19, 2015. www.managers-net.com/biography/mcgregor.html.

— — —. "George Elton Mayo." Accessed November 20, 2015. www.managers-net.com/Biography/Mayo.html.

Maslow, Abraham H. *Eupsychian Management*: *A Journal.* Homewood, IL: Irwin, 1965.

— — —. *Motivation and Personality*. New York: Harper & Row, 1954.

— — —."A Theory of Human Motivation." *Psychological Review* 50 (1943): 370–96.

McGregor, Douglas. "The Human Side of Enterprise." First published in *Adventure in Thought and Action*: Proceedings of the Fifth Anniversary Convocation of the School of Industrial Management, Massachusetts Institute of Technology, Cambridge, April 9, 1957. Cambridge, MA: MIT School of Industrial Management, 1957. Reprinted in *The Management Review* 46 (1957): 22–8.

————. *The Human Side of Enterprise*. New York: McGraw-Hill, 1960.

————. *The Professional Manager*. New York: McGraw-Hill, 1967.

McGregor Fund, "History." Accessed November 19, 2015. www.mcgregorfund. org/about-us/history.

Mind Tools Editorial Team. "Theory Z: Merging Eastern and Western Management Styles." Accessed November 24, 2015. www.mindtools.com/ pages/article/theory-z.htm

MIT Sloan School of Management. "Pioneered at MIT Sloan." Accessed November 19, 2015. mitsloan.mit.edu/faculty/spotlight/pioneered.php.

Ouchi, William G. *Theory Z: How American Business Can Meet the Japanese Challenge*. Reading, MA: Addison-Wesley, 1981.

Sanchez, Carol M., and Dawn M. Curtis, "Different Minds and Common Problems: Geert Hofstede's Research on National Cultures." *Performance Improvement Quarterly* 13, no. 2 (2000): 9–19.

Schein, Edgar. "In Defense of Theory Y." *Organizational Dynamics* 4 (1975): 17–30.

————. "Relationships between Sex Role Stereotypes and Requisite Management Characteristics among Female Managers." *Journal of Applied Psychology* 60, no. 3 (1975): 340–4.

Senge, Peter. *The Fifth Discipline: The Art and Practice of the Learning Organization.* New York: Doubleday, 1990.

————. "The Practice of Innovation." *Leader to Leader* 9 (1998): 16–22.

Sorensen, Peter F., and Matt Minahan. "McGregor's Legacy: The Evolution and Current Application of Theory Y Management." *Journal of Management History* 17, no. 2 (2011): 178–92.

Taylor, Frederick Winslow. "Fundamentals of Scientific Management." In *Working in America: Continuity, Conflict, and Change*, edited by Amy S. Wharton, 67–75. Mountain View, CA: Mayfield Publishing Company, 1998.

"The 25 Most Influential Business Management Books." *Time*. Accessed November 20, 2015. http://content.time.com/time/specials/packages/ completelist/0,29569,2086680,00.html.

Vaill, Peter B. "Process Wisdom for a New Age." *ReVISION* 7, no. 2 (1986): 39–49.

Waterman, Robert H. *The Frontiers of Excellence: Learning from Companies That Put People First*. London: Nicholas Brealey Publishing, 1994.

Watson, John B. "Psychology as the Behaviorist Views It." *Psychological Review* 20 (1913): 158–77.

Woodward, Joan. *Industrial Organization: Theory and Practice*. New York: Oxford University Press, 1965.

THE MACAT LIBRARY
BY DISCIPLINE

AFRICANA STUDIES

Chinua Achebe's *An Image of Africa: Racism in Conrad's Heart of Darkness*
W. E. B. Du Bois's *The Souls of Black Folk*
Zora Neale Huston's *Characteristics of Negro Expression*
Martin Luther King Jr's *Why We Can't Wait*
Toni Morrison's *Playing in the Dark: Whiteness in the American Literary Imagination*

ANTHROPOLOGY

Arjun Appadurai's *Modernity at Large: Cultural Dimensions of Globalisation*
Philippe Ariès's *Centuries of Childhood*
Franz Boas's *Race, Language and Culture*
Kim Chan & Renée Mauborgne's *Blue Ocean Strategy*
Jared Diamond's *Guns, Germs & Steel: the Fate of Human Societies*
Jared Diamond's *Collapse: How Societies Choose to Fail or Survive*
E. E. Evans-Pritchard's *Witchcraft, Oracles and Magic Among the Azande*
James Ferguson's *The Anti-Politics Machine*
Clifford Geertz's *The Interpretation of Cultures*
David Graeber's *Debt: the First 5000 Years*
Karen Ho's *Liquidated: An Ethnography of Wall Street*
Geert Hofstede's *Culture's Consequences: Comparing Values, Behaviors, Institutes and Organizations across Nations*
Claude Lévi-Strauss's *Structural Anthropology*
Jay Macleod's *Ain't No Makin' It: Aspirations and Attainment in a Low-Income Neighborhood*
Saba Mahmood's *The Politics of Piety: The Islamic Revival and the Feminist Subject*
Marcel Mauss's *The Gift*

BUSINESS

Jean Lave & Etienne Wenger's *Situated Learning*
Theodore Levitt's *Marketing Myopia*
Burton G. Malkiel's *A Random Walk Down Wall Street*
Douglas McGregor's *The Human Side of Enterprise*
Michael Porter's *Competitive Strategy: Creating and Sustaining Superior Performance*
John Kotter's *Leading Change*
C. K. Prahalad & Gary Hamel's *The Core Competence of the Corporation*

CRIMINOLOGY

Michelle Alexander's *The New Jim Crow: Mass Incarceration in the Age of Colorblindness*
Michael R. Gottfredson & Travis Hirschi's *A General Theory of Crime*
Richard Herrnstein & Charles A. Murray's *The Bell Curve: Intelligence and Class Structure in American Life*
Elizabeth Loftus's *Eyewitness Testimony*
Jay Macleod's *Ain't No Makin' It: Aspirations and Attainment in a Low-Income Neighborhood*
Philip Zimbardo's *The Lucifer Effect*

ECONOMICS

Janet Abu-Lughod's *Before European Hegemony*
Ha-Joon Chang's *Kicking Away the Ladder*
David Brion Davis's *The Problem of Slavery in the Age of Revolution*
Milton Friedman's *The Role of Monetary Policy*
Milton Friedman's *Capitalism and Freedom*
David Graeber's *Debt: the First 5000 Years*
Friedrich Hayek's *The Road to Serfdom*
Karen Ho's *Liquidated: An Ethnography of Wall Street*

John Maynard Keynes's *The General Theory of Employment, Interest and Money*
Charles P. Kindleberger's *Manias, Panics and Crashes*
Robert Lucas's *Why Doesn't Capital Flow from Rich to Poor Countries?*
Burton G. Malkiel's *A Random Walk Down Wall Street*
Thomas Robert Malthus's *An Essay on the Principle of Population*
Karl Marx's *Capital*
Thomas Piketty's *Capital in the Twenty-First Century*
Amartya Sen's *Development as Freedom*
Adam Smith's *The Wealth of Nations*
Nassim Nicholas Taleb's *The Black Swan: The Impact of the Highly Improbable*
Amos Tversky's & Daniel Kahneman's *Judgment under Uncertainty: Heuristics and Biases*
Mahbub Ul Haq's *Reflections on Human Development*
Max Weber's *The Protestant Ethic and the Spirit of Capitalism*

FEMINISM AND GENDER STUDIES

Judith Butler's *Gender Trouble*
Simone De Beauvoir's *The Second Sex*
Michel Foucault's *History of Sexuality*
Betty Friedan's *The Feminine Mystique*
Saba Mahmood's *The Politics of Piety: The Islamic Revival and the Feminist Subjec*t
Joan Wallach Scott's *Gender and the Politics of History*
Mary Wollstonecraft's *A Vindication of the Rights of Woman*
Virginia Woolf's *A Room of One's Own*

GEOGRAPHY

The Brundtland Report's *Our Common Future*
Rachel Carson's *Silent Spring*
Charles Darwin's *On the Origin of Species*
James Ferguson's *The Anti-Politics Machine*
Jane Jacobs's *The Death and Life of Great American Cities*
James Lovelock's *Gaia: A New Look at Life on Earth*
Amartya Sen's *Development as Freedom*
Mathis Wackernagel & William Rees's *Our Ecological Footprint*

HISTORY

Janet Abu-Lughod's *Before European Hegemony*
Benedict Anderson's *Imagined Communities*
Bernard Bailyn's *The Ideological Origins of the American Revolution*
Hanna Batatu's *The Old Social Classes And The Revolutionary Movements Of Iraq*
Christopher Browning's *Ordinary Men: Reserve Police Batallion 101 and the Final Solution in Poland*
Edmund Burke's *Reflections on the Revolution in France*
William Cronon's *Nature's Metropolis: Chicago And The Great West*
Alfred W. Crosby's *The Columbian Exchange*
Hamid Dabashi's *Iran: A People Interrupted*
David Brion Davis's *The Problem of Slavery in the Age of Revolution*
Nathalie Zemon Davis's *The Return of Martin Guerre*
Jared Diamond's *Guns, Germs & Steel: the Fate of Human Societies*
Frank Dikotter's *Mao's Great Famine*
John W Dower's *War Without Mercy: Race And Power In The Pacific War*
W. E. B. Du Bois's *The Souls of Black Folk*
Richard J. Evans's *In Defence of History*
Lucien Febvre's *The Problem of Unbelief in the 16th Century*
Sheila Fitzpatrick's *Everyday Stalinism*

The Macat Library By Discipline

Eric Foner's *Reconstruction: America's Unfinished Revolution, 1863-1877*
Michel Foucault's *Discipline and Punish*
Michel Foucault's *History of Sexuality*
Francis Fukuyama's *The End of History and the Last Man*
John Lewis Gaddis's *We Now Know: Rethinking Cold War History*
Ernest Gellner's *Nations and Nationalism*
Eugene Genovese's *Roll, Jordan, Roll: The World the Slaves Made*
Carlo Ginzburg's *The Night Battles*
Daniel Goldhagen's *Hitler's Willing Executioners*
Jack Goldstone's *Revolution and Rebellion in the Early Modern World*
Antonio Gramsci's *The Prison Notebooks*
Alexander Hamilton, John Jay & James Madison's *The Federalist Papers*
Christopher Hill's *The World Turned Upside Down*
Carole Hillenbrand's *The Crusades: Islamic Perspectives*
Thomas Hobbes's *Leviathan*
Eric Hobsbawm's *The Age Of Revolution*
John A. Hobson's *Imperialism: A Study*
Albert Hourani's *History of the Arab Peoples*
Samuel P. Huntington's *The Clash of Civilizations and the Remaking of World Order*
C. L. R. James's *The Black Jacobins*
Tony Judt's *Postwar: A History of Europe Since 1945*
Ernst Kantorowicz's *The King's Two Bodies: A Study in Medieval Political Theology*
Paul Kennedy's *The Rise and Fall of the Great Powers*
Ian Kershaw's *The "Hitler Myth": Image and Reality in the Third Reich*
John Maynard Keynes's *The General Theory of Employment, Interest and Money*
Charles P. Kindleberger's *Manias, Panics and Crashes*
Martin Luther King Jr's *Why We Can't Wait*
Henry Kissinger's *World Order: Reflections on the Character of Nations and the Course of History*
Thomas Kuhn's *The Structure of Scientific Revolutions*
Georges Lefebvre's *The Coming of the French Revolution*
John Locke's *Two Treatises of Government*
Niccolò Machiavelli's *The Prince*
Thomas Robert Malthus's *An Essay on the Principle of Population*
Mahmood Mamdani's *Citizen and Subject: Contemporary Africa And The Legacy Of Late Colonialism*
Karl Marx's *Capital*
Stanley Milgram's *Obedience to Authority*
John Stuart Mill's *On Liberty*
Thomas Paine's *Common Sense*
Thomas Paine's *Rights of Man*
Geoffrey Parker's *Global Crisis: War, Climate Change and Catastrophe in the Seventeenth Century*
Jonathan Riley-Smith's *The First Crusade and the Idea of Crusading*
Jean-Jacques Rousseau's *The Social Contract*
Joan Wallach Scott's *Gender and the Politics of History*
Theda Skocpol's *States and Social Revolutions*
Adam Smith's *The Wealth of Nations*
Timothy Snyder's *Bloodlands: Europe Between Hitler and Stalin*
Sun Tzu's *The Art of War*
Keith Thomas's *Religion and the Decline of Magic*
Thucydides's *The History of the Peloponnesian War*
Frederick Jackson Turner's *The Significance of the Frontier in American History*
Odd Arne Westad's *The Global Cold War: Third World Interventions And The Making Of Our Times*

LITERATURE

Chinua Achebe's *An Image of Africa: Racism in Conrad's Heart of Darkness*
Roland Barthes's *Mythologies*
Homi K. Bhabha's *The Location of Culture*
Judith Butler's *Gender Trouble*
Simone De Beauvoir's *The Second Sex*
Ferdinand De Saussure's *Course in General Linguistics*
T. S. Eliot's *The Sacred Wood: Essays on Poetry and Criticism*
Zora Neale Huston's *Characteristics of Negro Expression*
Toni Morrison's *Playing in the Dark: Whiteness in the American Literary Imagination*
Edward Said's *Orientalism*
Gayatri Chakravorty Spivak's *Can the Subaltern Speak?*
Mary Wollstonecraft's *A Vindication of the Rights of Women*
Virginia Woolf's *A Room of One's Own*

PHILOSOPHY

Elizabeth Anscombe's *Modern Moral Philosophy*
Hannah Arendt's *The Human Condition*
Aristotle's *Metaphysics*
Aristotle's *Nicomachean Ethics*
Edmund Gettier's *Is Justified True Belief Knowledge?*
Georg Wilhelm Friedrich Hegel's *Phenomenology of Spirit*
David Hume's *Dialogues Concerning Natural Religion*
David Hume's *The Enquiry for Human Understanding*
Immanuel Kant's *Religion within the Boundaries of Mere Reason*
Immanuel Kant's *Critique of Pure Reason*
Søren Kierkegaard's *The Sickness Unto Death*
Søren Kierkegaard's *Fear and Trembling*
C. S. Lewis's *The Abolition of Man*
Alasdair MacIntyre's *After Virtue*
Marcus Aurelius's *Meditations*
Friedrich Nietzsche's *On the Genealogy of Morality*
Friedrich Nietzsche's *Beyond Good and Evil*
Plato's *Republic*
Plato's *Symposium*
Jean-Jacques Rousseau's *The Social Contract*
Gilbert Ryle's *The Concept of Mind*
Baruch Spinoza's *Ethics*
Sun Tzu's *The Art of War*
Ludwig Wittgenstein's *Philosophical Investigations*

POLITICS

Benedict Anderson's *Imagined Communities*
Aristotle's *Politics*
Bernard Bailyn's *The Ideological Origins of the American Revolution*
Edmund Burke's *Reflections on the Revolution in France*
John C. Calhoun's *A Disquisition on Government*
Ha-Joon Chang's *Kicking Away the Ladder*
Hamid Dabashi's *Iran: A People Interrupted*
Hamid Dabashi's *Theology of Discontent: The Ideological Foundation of the Islamic Revolution in Iran*
Robert Dahl's *Democracy and its Critics*
Robert Dahl's *Who Governs?*
David Brion Davis's *The Problem of Slavery in the Age of Revolution*

The Macat Library By Discipline

Alexis De Tocqueville's *Democracy in America*
James Ferguson's *The Anti-Politics Machine*
Frank Dikotter's *Mao's Great Famine*
Sheila Fitzpatrick's *Everyday Stalinism*
Eric Foner's *Reconstruction: America's Unfinished Revolution, 1863-1877*
Milton Friedman's *Capitalism and Freedom*
Francis Fukuyama's *The End of History and the Last Man*
John Lewis Gaddis's *We Now Know: Rethinking Cold War History*
Ernest Gellner's *Nations and Nationalism*
David Graeber's *Debt: the First 5000 Years*
Antonio Gramsci's *The Prison Notebooks*
Alexander Hamilton, John Jay & James Madison's *The Federalist Papers*
Friedrich Hayek's *The Road to Serfdom*
Christopher Hill's *The World Turned Upside Down*
Thomas Hobbes's *Leviathan*
John A. Hobson's *Imperialism: A Study*
Samuel P. Huntington's *The Clash of Civilizations and the Remaking of World Order*
Tony Judt's *Postwar: A History of Europe Since 1945*
David C. Kang's *China Rising: Peace, Power and Order in East Asia*
Paul Kennedy's *The Rise and Fall of Great Powers*
Robert Keohane's *After Hegemony*
Martin Luther King Jr.'s *Why We Can't Wait*
Henry Kissinger's *World Order: Reflections on the Character of Nations and the Course of History*
John Locke's *Two Treatises of Government*
Niccolò Machiavelli's *The Prince*
Thomas Robert Malthus's *An Essay on the Principle of Population*
Mahmood Mamdani's *Citizen and Subject: Contemporary Africa And The Legacy Of Late Colonialism*
Karl Marx's *Capital*
John Stuart Mill's *On Liberty*
John Stuart Mill's *Utilitarianism*
Hans Morgenthau's *Politics Among Nations*
Thomas Paine's *Common Sense*
Thomas Paine's *Rights of Man*
Thomas Piketty's *Capital in the Twenty-First Century*
Robert D. Putman's *Bowling Alone*
John Rawls's *Theory of Justice*
Jean-Jacques Rousseau's *The Social Contract*
Theda Skocpol's *States and Social Revolutions*
Adam Smith's *The Wealth of Nations*
Sun Tzu's *The Art of War*
Henry David Thoreau's *Civil Disobedience*
Thucydides's *The History of the Peloponnesian War*
Kenneth Waltz's *Theory of International Politics*
Max Weber's *Politics as a Vocation*
Odd Arne Westad's *The Global Cold War: Third World Interventions And The Making Of Our Times*

POSTCOLONIAL STUDIES

Roland Barthes's *Mythologies*
Frantz Fanon's *Black Skin, White Masks*
Homi K. Bhabha's *The Location of Culture*
Gustavo Gutiérrez's *A Theology of Liberation*
Edward Said's *Orientalism*
Gayatri Chakravorty Spivak's *Can the Subaltern Speak?*

PSYCHOLOGY

Gordon Allport's *The Nature of Prejudice*
Alan Baddeley & Graham Hitch's *Aggression: A Social Learning Analysis*
Albert Bandura's *Aggression: A Social Learning Analysis*
Leon Festinger's *A Theory of Cognitive Dissonance*
Sigmund Freud's *The Interpretation of Dreams*
Betty Friedan's *The Feminine Mystique*
Michael R. Gottfredson & Travis Hirschi's *A General Theory of Crime*
Eric Hoffer's *The True Believer: Thoughts on the Nature of Mass Movements*
William James's *Principles of Psychology*
Elizabeth Loftus's *Eyewitness Testimony*
A. H. Maslow's *A Theory of Human Motivation*
Stanley Milgram's *Obedience to Authority*
Steven Pinker's *The Better Angels of Our Nature*
Oliver Sacks's *The Man Who Mistook His Wife For a Hat*
Richard Thaler & Cass Sunstein's *Nudge: Improving Decisions About Health, Wealth and Happiness*
Amos Tversky's *Judgment under Uncertainty: Heuristics and Biases*
Philip Zimbardo's *The Lucifer Effect*

SCIENCE

Rachel Carson's *Silent Spring*
William Cronon's *Nature's Metropolis: Chicago And The Great West*
Alfred W. Crosby's *The Columbian Exchange*
Charles Darwin's *On the Origin of Species*
Richard Dawkin's *The Selfish Gene*
Thomas Kuhn's *The Structure of Scientific Revolutions*
Geoffrey Parker's *Global Crisis: War, Climate Change and Catastrophe in the Seventeenth Century*
Mathis Wackernagel & William Rees's *Our Ecological Footprint*

SOCIOLOGY

Michelle Alexander's *The New Jim Crow: Mass Incarceration in the Age of Colorblindness*
Gordon Allport's *The Nature of Prejudice*
Albert Bandura's *Aggression: A Social Learning Analysis*
Hanna Batatu's *The Old Social Classes And The Revolutionary Movements Of Iraq*
Ha-Joon Chang's *Kicking Away the Ladder*
W. E. B. Du Bois's *The Souls of Black Folk*
Émile Durkheim's *On Suicide*
Frantz Fanon's *Black Skin, White Masks*
Frantz Fanon's *The Wretched of the Earth*
Eric Foner's *Reconstruction: America's Unfinished Revolution, 1863-1877*
Eugene Genovese's *Roll, Jordan, Roll: The World the Slaves Made*
Jack Goldstone's *Revolution and Rebellion in the Early Modern World*
Antonio Gramsci's *The Prison Notebooks*
Richard Herrnstein & Charles A Murray's *The Bell Curve: Intelligence and Class Structure in American Life*
Eric Hoffer's *The True Believer: Thoughts on the Nature of Mass Movements*
Jane Jacobs's *The Death and Life of Great American Cities*
Robert Lucas's *Why Doesn't Capital Flow from Rich to Poor Countries?*
Jay Macleod's *Ain't No Makin' It: Aspirations and Attainment in a Low Income Neighborhood*
Elaine May's *Homeward Bound: American Families in the Cold War Era*
Douglas McGregor's *The Human Side of Enterprise*
C. Wright Mills's *The Sociological Imagination*

Thomas Piketty's *Capital in the Twenty-First Century*
Robert D. Putman's *Bowling Alone*
David Riesman's *The Lonely Crowd: A Study of the Changing American Character*
Edward Said's *Orientalism*
Joan Wallach Scott's *Gender and the Politics of History*
Theda Skocpol's *States and Social Revolutions*
Max Weber's *The Protestant Ethic and the Spirit of Capitalism*

THEOLOGY

Augustine's *Confessions*
Benedict's *Rule of St Benedict*
Gustavo Gutiérrez's *A Theology of Liberation*
Carole Hillenbrand's *The Crusades: Islamic Perspectives*
David Hume's *Dialogues Concerning Natural Religion*
Immanuel Kant's *Religion within the Boundaries of Mere Reason*
Ernst Kantorowicz's *The King's Two Bodies: A Study in Medieval Political Theology*
Søren Kierkegaard's *The Sickness Unto Death*
C. S. Lewis's *The Abolition of Man*
Saba Mahmood's *The Politics of Piety: The Islamic Revival and the Feminist Subject*
Baruch Spinoza's *Ethics*
Keith Thomas's *Religion and the Decline of Magic*

COMING SOON

Chris Argyris's *The Individual and the Organisation*
Seyla Benhabib's *The Rights of Others*
Walter Benjamin's *The Work Of Art in the Age of Mechanical Reproduction*
John Berger's *Ways of Seeing*
Pierre Bourdieu's *Outline of a Theory of Practice*
Mary Douglas's *Purity and Danger*
Roland Dworkin's *Taking Rights Seriously*
James G. March's *Exploration and Exploitation in Organisational Learning*
Ikujiro Nonaka's *A Dynamic Theory of Organizational Knowledge Creation*
Griselda Pollock's *Vision and Difference*
Amartya Sen's *Inequality Re-Examined*
Susan Sontag's *On Photography*
Yasser Tabbaa's *The Transformation of Islamic Art*
Ludwig von Mises's *Theory of Money and Credit*

Macat Disciplines

Access the greatest ideas and thinkers across entire disciplines, including

FEMINISM, GENDER AND QUEER STUDIES

Simone De Beauvoir's
The Second Sex

Michel Foucault's
History of Sexuality

Betty Friedan's
The Feminine Mystique

Saba Mahmood's
The Politics of Piety: The Islamic Revival and the Feminist Subject

Joan Wallach Scott's
Gender and the Politics of History

Mary Wollstonecraft's
A Vindication of the Rights of Woman

Virginia Woolf's
A Room of One's Own

Judith Butler's
Gender Trouble

Macat analyses are available from all good bookshops and libraries.

Access hundreds of analyses through one, multimedia tool.
Join free for one month **library.macat.com**

Macat Disciplines

Access the greatest ideas and thinkers across entire disciplines, including

CRIMINOLOGY

Michelle Alexander's
The New Jim Crow: Mass Incarceration in the Age of Colorblindness

Michael R. Gottfredson & Travis Hirschi's
A General Theory of Crime

Elizabeth Loftus's
Eyewitness Testimony

Richard Herrnstein & Charles A. Murray's
The Bell Curve: Intelligence and Class Structure in American Life

Jay Macleod's
Ain't No Makin' It: Aspirations and Attainment in a Low-Income Neighborhood

Philip Zimbardo's
The Lucifer Effect

Macat analyses are available from all good bookshops and libraries.

Access hundreds of analyses through one, multimedia tool.
Join free for one month **library.macat.com**

Macat Disciplines

Access the greatest ideas and thinkers across entire disciplines, including

Postcolonial Studies

Roland Barthes's *Mythologies*
Frantz Fanon's *Black Skin, White Masks*
Homi K. Bhabha's *The Location of Culture*
Gustavo Gutiérrez's *A Theology of Liberation*
Edward Said's *Orientalism*
Gayatri Chakravorty Spivak's *Can the Subaltern Speak?*

Macat analyses are available from all good bookshops and libraries.

Access hundreds of analyses through one, multimedia tool.
Join free for one month **library.macat.com**

Macat Disciplines

Access the greatest ideas and thinkers across entire disciplines, including

GLOBALIZATION

Arjun Appadurai's, *Modernity at Large: Cultural Dimensions of Globalisation*

James Ferguson's, *The Anti-Politics Machine*

Geert Hofstede's, *Culture's Consequences*

Amartya Sen's, *Development as Freedom*

Macat analyses are available from all good bookshops and libraries.

Access hundreds of analyses through one, multimedia tool.
Join free for one month **library.macat.com**

Macat Pairs

*Analyse historical and modern issues
from opposite sides of an argument.
Pairs include:*

HOW TO RUN AN ECONOMY

John Maynard Keynes's
*The General Theory OF Employment,
Interest and Money*

Classical economics suggests that market economies
are self-correcting in times of recession or depression,
and tend toward full employment and output. But
English economist John Maynard Keynes disagrees.

In his ground-breaking 1936 study *The General
Theory*, Keynes argues that traditional economics
has misunderstood the causes of unemployment.
Employment is not determined by the price of labor;
it is directly linked to demand. Keynes believes market
economies are by nature unstable, and so require
government intervention. Spurred on by the social
catastrophe of the Great Depression of the 1930s,
he sets out to revolutionize the way the world thinks

Milton Friedman's
The Role of Monetary Policy

Friedman's 1968 paper changed the course of
economic theory. In just 17 pages, he demolished
existing theory and outlined an effective alternate
monetary policy designed to secure 'high employment,
stable prices and rapid growth.'

Friedman demonstrated that monetary policy plays
a vital role in broader economic stability and argued
that economists got their monetary policy wrong
in the 1950s and 1960s by misunderstanding the
relationship between inflation and unemployment.
Previous generations of economists had believed
that governments could permanently decrease
unemployment by permitting inflation—and vice versa.
Friedman's most original contribution was to show that
this supposed trade-off is an illusion that only works in
the short term.

Macat Pairs

Analyse historical and modern issues
and opposite sides of an argument.
Pairs series

Printed in the United States
by Baker & Taylor Publisher Services